How to Read a Novel

A USER'S GUIDE

John Sutherland

P

PROFILE BOOKS

This paperback edition published in 2007

First published in Great Britain in 2006 by
Profile Books Ltd
3A Exmouth House
Pine Street
Exmouth Market
London EC1R 0JH
www.profilebooks.com

10 9 8 7 6 5 4 3 2

Text design by Sue Lamble

Typeset in Quadraat by MacGuru Ltd
info@macguru.org.uk

Printed in the UK by CPI Bookmarque, Croydon, CR0 4TD

A CIP catalogue record for this book is available from the British Library.

ISBN 978 1 86197 986 5

Contents

How to Read a Novel

Introduction

I RECALL ONE evening walking to the underground with A. S. Byatt, after a day's teaching. We were both then lecturers in the same English Department. Why, I asked, did she publish so much higher journalism: I couldn't open a copy of a literary supplement or an opinion-forming magazine without seeing her name. It was great stuff, but why so much?

'Because I need shoes,' she replied, dryly, 'and I like to buy new ones from time to time.' She then went off to get her train to Wandsworth.

Nowadays the author of *Possession* could outbuy Imelda Marcos − were she so inclined. Probably Wandsworth, too. And when she writes (she still does a lot of it), I suspect, Dame Antonia now writes for herself: not for shoe-leather. And very well she writes.

Most authors' motives are impure. (What was it Byron said: 'money, fame, and the love of beautiful women'?) My motives in writing *How to Read a Novel* were, I admit, mixed. No beautiful women, alas. Shoes? Perhaps.

The main motive, the worm in my apple, was embarrassment. Embarrassment, that is, at how little fiction I've read, set against the mass there is to read. It's the familiar 'so many novels, so little time' problem. It's also an insoluble problem.

The stuff spills out faster than one can even read the listings of what one will never get round to reading. Every time one logs on to amazon there's another half million – all yours for a click and a flash of plastic. The buying experience has sped up to a matter of nano-seconds, while reading practice is something else: even the most practised reader of fiction will be doing well to manage a page a minute.

One can, of course, as recommended by the witty Frenchman Pierre Bayard whose *Comment parler des livres que l'on na pas lus?* (*How to Talk about Books One Hasn't Read*) was published in 2007, go in for the higher bluffery. Bayard shrewdly points out, since the person (or class) you're talking to won't probably have read the book either you can usually fake it. But, possibly, someone *will* have read what you haven't and are talking about, with all the confidence of the consummate un-reader. Sod's law applies to literary conversation as much as to anything else in life. At one's back one always hears the whirring of the bullshit meter (is there a French word for 'bullshit'? How about 'sod's law'?)

How best to invest one's tiny mite: the (say) 1,001 novels one can read in a lifetime? Our current addiction to 'best ever', 'must read', 'bestseller' lists, charts and tables reflects that anxiety. This taxonomic desperation originated, literary historians record, in the 1890s, at exactly the same time, as the historians elsewhere record, that the number of new novels produced annually began to overflow the containers society has for them.

As a number of reviewers pointed out (some indulgently, others less so) *How to Read a Novel* did not, in any detail, instruct on how to read so much as how to position oneself to undertake that act. How, as it were, to close in on the novel, fending off commercial coercion, word-of-mouth seductions, the herd instinct to thunder along behind the crowd – above all, how to dig out the right book from the huge mass available.

An ever increasing mass. On the day I'm writing this, *Forbes Magazine* proclaims last year to have been the richest ever for the human race. I would wager that, for English Language readers, 2006–7 was also the richest-ever year for fiction. And, for a certainty, 2008 will be even richer. This is not merely a function of ever more new novels as the fact that – unlike other products – old novels do not disappear once consumed; like old soldiers, they never fade away. The must-read archive gets bigger and bigger. Bestseller lists used to contain ten titles, now it's up to a hundred. It's like a mountain which grows faster than any reader can climb. How to be well-read in the twenty-first century? Can one be well-read?

As the sad witness of lottery winners testifies, vast wealth seldom makes life easier. We are, as regards the range, quality and sheer number of novels available to us in 2007, better off than all generations before us. 'Embarrassment' is inadequate to describe the dilemmas this unprecedented richness poses. It is not (as it was in my youth) disposable cash which defines the dilemma, but available time. We live longer than we did but even if we lasted as long as Swift's Struldbrugs the reader's eye would never catch up with the writer's hand.

A related, more intractable, and perennially fascinating issue is why we *need* so much narrative in our lives. It's not just novels. Why is it that 100 per cent of what is shown on our cinema screens, over 50 percent on our TV screens is fictional narrative. Even newspaper and magazine articles are sucked, inexorably, to the condition of 'stories' with beginnings, middles, and ends.

Why, in a life where (as a modern Gradgrind would

say), Fact is paramount, hurry incessant and the real world so pressing do we crave such large, time-wasting doses of fiction? Dickens, the creator of Gradgrind, proposes one answer: 'people muth't be amuth'd', as the circus-master Sleary (rather too liquidly in my view) insists.

Imagination, Dickens argues, must be fed if we are to live full lives: deny that nourishment and life shrivels. Man does not live by fact alone. One of the novelist's targets in Hard Times (along with the political economists, the utilitarians, and Preston's striking textile workers) was the anti-fiction prejudice of the newly founded public libraries in Britain.

The public library battle has been well won. The novel triumphs on its shelves. But, in the interwar years of the twentieth century, fiction faced an even sterner cultural test than the stony faced public librarian. How could reading novels justify itself as a university subject? Belletrism – the notion that fictional prose was an art which connoisseurs could relish like fine wine was deemed to be beneath the level of an academic 'discipline'; too weak-wristed. Something strenuous was required, something as strenuous as Anglo Saxon, or classics.

From Cambridge University came a saving strategy – a way of reading novels as 'critically' as philologists read the Ormulum or chemists turned blue litmus paper red. Fiction, the new puritans of reading declared, had two contrary characters. The first (wholly deleterious) was escapist. The novel, like gin, was the shortest way out of Manchester, or wherever. On its wings, little Wellsian people, leading their little lives, could drug themselves into accepting those little lives. The mill-girl, dosing herself with regular drams of romance from Peg's Paper or the Kippsian counter-jumper with a 'shilling shocker' stuck in his hip pocket, was the image associated with this fiction. Critical sneer was the approved dismissive technique.

There was, however, another worthier kind of fiction which offered engagement, not escape, from the real world. These novels lent readers (the relatively few capable of profiting from the loan) the privilege of sharing a superior sensibility: seeing the real world through other eyes which rendered the world more, not less, real. The trick was to separate one kind of novel from the other. The faculty required for this operation was 'discrimination'. The critical razor, applied to the mass, could find the vein of gold among the mountainous dross.

Famously the Leavises, with whom this harsh doctrine is principally associated, found room on their bookshelves for only a yard or two of truly worthwhile works (together with the yard or two of their own – justifying the first yard). The avatar was D. H. Lawrence. The stricter sect of Leavisites held to the belief that after Lawrence there was nothing. The rim of the fictional universe had been reached with *Women in Love*.

It was an intellectually gratifying, and highly economic doctrine, but radically ungenerous. Those who, like myself, were subjected to it in the decades that its parsimony dominated university study of fiction felt that it left one culturally airless. There was all that activity, elsewhere, which one was prohibited from even thinking about.

In recent years, more relaxed, and intellectually curious academic disciplines (notably literary sociology, and media studies) have widened the gate from its Leavisian straitness. I have even read answers on Jackie Collins in finals papers, and (many, many) dissertations on graphic fiction. Neil Gaiman is now scrutinised as rigorously as was once the artist-prophet of Eastwood.

But the big questions remain. Why so many novels? How

should we (can we) deal with them? Why do we need them? And, if we need them, how do we make the necessary moves so as to invest our reading time wisely.

There are, I think, no easy answers. My own view is that with the rise of the novel (as Ian Watt memorably called it) in the eighteenth century, human consciousness was as revolutionised as it was by Watt and steam power, by the 1832 Reform Act and the extension of the franchise, or even (to be personal) by the 1963 Higher Education Robbins Report.

With mass access to fiction it became legitimate for any literate persons, of any class, to fantasise infinite possibilities, and to feed those possibilities back into their own lives. That life became larger and more potential.

Making the right choices, however, as in all other defining areas of life remains life's most difficult thing. Not least, I would argue, with the novels one chooses as companions along the way.

Post Script

I am grateful to reviewers who were kind about the first edition of HTRAN (as Profile abbreviated the title, for in-house reference). I kiss the rod of those who weren't so kind – especially those who were good enough to point out errors which are (I trust) here corrected. A couple of the unkind ones were so amusing about me that, if I hadn't been the author, I would have split my sides laughing.

The blogosphere was very taken with the page 69 test, and one site (in defiance of porn-sites' affection for the digits) actually named itself in honour of Marshall McCluhan's dipstick technique. Another blogsite double-decked itself by adding a page 99 test (which it attributed to the novelist

Ford Madox Ford – something I did not know). As a number of commentators pointed out, however, page 69 was not the jewel in the HTRAN crown, as published in hardback. I have instructed Profile to take note, in resetting the book. Page 99 I leave to its chances and any readers I am lucky enough to find.

John Sutherland
May 2007

chapter 1

So many novels, so little time

AN ALTERNATIVE TITLE for this book might be *Reading in an Age of Plenty* or, more eye-catchingly, *Reading through the Avalanche*. In part it's an autobiographical exercise. During my novel-reading lifetime (1943 to 2006 and still going) the national book supply has swollen from trickle to deluge, with the prospect of a veritable tsunami to come. Every week now more novels are published than Samuel Johnson had to deal with in a decade.

If you had the riches of Croesus (or Bill Gates) you could, with a few hours' key-stroking, order up from Amazon. com some half-million novels to be Fedexed, rush delivery, in thirty-six hours. You would, of course, need a disused airplane hangar to keep the books in and a small army of forklifting stackers and fetchers to move the things. Given a reading career of fifty years, a 40-hour reading week, a 46-week working year and three hours per novel, you would, as I calculate, need 163 lifetimes to read them all. And very dull lifetimes they would be. More fun on the forklifts.

Ornithologists can, and do, observe with their own eyes up to 90 per cent of the globe's 9,000 or so surviving birds, but no one in the twenty-first century is going to scrape away at more than a tiny fraction of the fiction that is on offer – the fiction that is just a keystroke and a Fedex delivery away; or, if push comes to shove, a visit to the nearest copyright or major university library.

It is that condition of surplusage which is the *raison d'être* of this book about books. Targeting, archiving and reading techniques have necessarily evolved with the daunting amount of fiction-reading experience now on offer. And, as I have already stressed, the relative shortness of time in which the modern reader has to read. To have enjoyed Goncharov, Tolstoy, Dostoyevsky and Turgenev, V. S. Pritchett once mused, the Russian day must surely have been longer – like those summertime White Nights in St Petersburg, when the sun barely sets. How else could the nineteenth-century Russian have done justice to the massiveness of *War and Peace*, *Crime and Punishment*, or *Oblomov* (itself, incidentally, a comic fantasia on vast tracts of time, with nothing to do but lie on a sofa and consume fiction and food)? Time must surely have ticked slower for Tolstoy's contemporaries. Pritchett , a practitioner of exquisite short fiction, inhabited a more hurried world.

Russians of the reading classes indeed had enviable amenities – notably more leisure time and more servants. And, in summer, the days *were* longer which spared candles and eyestrain. Most importantly, there were fewer novels to deal with. Anna Karenina, who read the congenially spacious Trollope on her journey from Moscow back to St Petersburg, had her first-class seat comfortably set up for her, with a special reading lamp, by her servant in a ladies only compartment. If she dropped her Trollope to the carriage floor, Annushka was there to pick the volume up for her (only twenty years earlier, it would have been a serf). The passage from *Anna Karenina* (1873–7) is worth quoting in its entirety for the sublimely languorous description of the Russian reading experience, AD 1870:

With the same preoccupied mind she had had all that day, Anna prepared with pleasure and great deliberation for the journey. With her deft little hands she unlocked her red bag, took out a small pillow which she placed against her knees, and locked the bag again; then she carefully wrapped up her feet and sat down comfortably. An invalid lady was already going to bed [this, remember, is a railway carriage]. Two other ladies began talking to Anna. One, a fat old woman, while wrapping up her feet, remarked upon the heating of the carriage. Anna said a few words in answer, but not foreseeing anything interesting from the conversation asked her maid to get out her reading lamp, fixed it to the arm of her seat, and took a paper knife and an English novel from her handbag. At first she could not read. For a while the bustle of people moving about disturbed her, and when the train had finally started it was impossible not to listen to the noises; then there was the snow, beating against the window on her left, to which it stuck, and the sight of the guard, who passed through the carriage closely wrapped up and covered with snow on one side; also the conversation about the awful snow-storm which was raging outside distracted her attention. And so it went on and on: the same jolting and knocking, the same beating of the snow on the window-pane, the same rapid changes from steaming heat to cold, and back again to heat, the gleam of the same faces through the semi-darkness, and the same voices, – but at last Anna began to read and to follow what she read. Annushka was already dozing, her broad hands, with a hole in one of the gloves, holding the red bag on her lap. Anna read and understood, but it was unpleasant to read, that is to say, to follow the reflection of other people's lives. She was too eager to live herself. When she read how the heroine of the novel nursed a sick man, she wanted to move about the sick room with noiseless footsteps; when she read of a member of Parliament making a speech, she wished to make that speech; when she read how Lady Mary rode to hounds, teased her sister-in-law, and astonished everybody by her boldness – she wanted to do it herself. But there was nothing to be done, so she forced herself to read, while her little hand played with the smooth paper knife.[1]

Picture Anna Karenina in her carriage the next time you ride a crowded, sweaty underground train or subway car, alongside some passenger cramming in a couple of pages of Danielle Steel, or John Grisham, before their stop. And it would be wiser, given recent terrorist outrages, not to start wielding your smooth paper knife in the carriage.

To be 'well read' in Britain or America in 1906 was to have a good library, a good source of literary news (Lord Northcliffe's new publication, The Times Literary Supplement, for example; or, for Americans, Harry Thurston Peck's the Bookman), access to a good bookstore and friends in the know about what 'everyone' was reading. And, of course, lots of time. It was manageable. A person could be well read and still have a life.

No longer. To be 'well read' in 2006 requires non-traditional strategies and ruthless short cuts. When, as is now imminent, the whole of print goes on line, new, more drastic

strategies will be required. In 2016, the ratio of fiction accessible to time available will be, frankly, mind-boggling. Mind
rupturing might be the more accurate term. As reported in
the *Guardian*, Bill Gates, on a stopover in the United Kingdom
in October 2005, predicted that

> the next challenge would be to take advantage of ubiqui-
> tous wireless, super-fast internet connections. Advances
> in computer hardware had been a 'miracle' but high-speed
> internet connections would accelerate the pace of change
> even further. Computers would become almost invisible,
> he said, integrated into everything that we do. 'In some
> ways the computer just disappears into the environment.
> All these devices will be hooked up to the internet and the
> internet will not have any speed limitations. And these
> devices will be a lot cheaper than they are today,' he said.
> Magazines and newspapers would eventually become
> redundant in their existing form, with interactive, person-
> alised content delivered to handheld devices. 'A lot of the
> reading that's taking place, the richness to be able to call
> up anything will take over,' he said. Mr Gates pointed
> to students as an example of how the world would shift
> from books to bytes. 'Within four or five years, instead of
> spending money on textbooks they'll spend a mere $400
> or so buying that tablet device and the material they hook
> up to will all be on the wireless internet with animations,
> timelines and links to deep information. But they'll be
> spending less than they would have on text books and
> have a dramatically better experience.'

Like Moses, the supernerd of Seattle descends from
Mount Rainier with the tablets that will transform not just the
reading practices of students but of novel lovers – although
from now on, their beloved novels will be made of silicon

and plastic. Consumers will be able to retrieve every work of fiction ever printed, instantly, in whatever typeface, font size and page layout they like.

Techno-Utopia is not merely a question of storage – more books and bigger attics. Gates's techno-adept (probably young) reader of the future will be able call up, out of the trillions of words which have survived their moment in print, exactly those words which s/he wants. No pudding but will give up its plum in a nanosecond. Anna Karenina, AD 2016, will be able, should she be curious on the subject, to summon up every novel with an English baronet for a hero in the entire library of English fiction with a couple of keystrokes. And a small fee, of course, to Microsoft Inc. Just because it is easy does not mean it is free.

It is possible to have too much of every good thing. Novels are no exception. In the past getting books, or access to books, was the problem. Today the problem is staggering out from under the book avalanche. Chaucer's clerk, ancestor to Bill Gates's tablet-wielding student of the near future, had, the poet informs us, one little row of books (manuscript books, presumably; Master Caxton's apparatus being decades in the future) on the shelf above his head. It was, Chaucer leads us to believe, a massive library by the standards of the day – the bibliographical equivalent of Michael Jackson's six Rolls-Royces. Something to draw wondering attention. Chaucer's clerk would have known his books by heart, for memorisation was a key element of a scholar's education in the pre-print era, as was the 'lecture' – one person reading the only book around for the benefit of the bookless many. The practice survives, anachronistically, in modern universities – Bill Gates will doubtless do for that as well with microelectronic lecture bots implanted in the student cranium.

The modern clerk, AD 2010, or not long thereafter, will have millions of books, and growing, on his virtual shelf. Memory will be a silicon chip hardly bigger than a grain of sand and a search engine, faster in its global circuits than Ariel. How to navigate that ocean of print? Historically, over the last few decades, the gradual trend for those wishing conscientiously to *choose* their books – rather than have them rammed down their throats, as Strasbourg geese are stuffed with liver-splitting fodder – has been away from 'discrimination' towards 'zap and scrap'. Selecting one's reading matter is less important nowadays than deselecting it. And even that term is too tame, suggesting as it does judicious shall-I, shan't-I? decision making. The modern reader is like an explorer cutting his way through the jungle with a machete – slashing a path to that single volume which is, just now, wanted.

It is not that life is too short to read carefully: the task is too great to be done attentively. One simply cannot keep abreast, any more than the sorcerer's apprentice could. The signals emanating from the bookshop (high street or webstore variety) are confusing, coercive and culturally deafening. Hype, celebrity authorship, high-pressure sales tactics ('3 for 2', '£6 off', 'NYT #1 Bestseller'), billboard advertisements, big name endorsements, dumpbins, eye-catching covers and dust-jackets embellished with glowing endorsements – all combine to induce consumer automatism. This, of course, is precisely what the industry wants. Retailers see nothing horrific in customers being forcefed like the Strasbourg geese, any more than do the goose farmers of Strasbourg their poultry. And doubtless Stepford's Borders and Barnes and Noble are the happiest booksellers in Connecticut.

On the customer's part, playing the stuffed goose will

often have its appeal. When there is such a superfluity of choice, and so many confusing stimuli, the natural inclination is to fall back on reflexive, unthinking purchase. Hit the nerve and the knee jumps. Take what is most drastically marked down, what is nearest, what is shouting loudest at you, what every one else is reading, what the person next to you on the tube was reading this morning, what the talk show host was boosting on the breakfast programme. Go for the franchised product – I loved Colin Firth in the movie (that nippled shirt!), *Pride and Prejudice* looks hard going and has some uncomfortable overtones of A-level. Let's buy *The Jane Austen Dating Book*. Anything rather than *choose*. The choices are already made. Only the purchasing remains to be done. Plastic has made that as easy as pressing a button.

And if one must read a classic, go for whatever Andrew Davies is adapting this season, or whichever Jane Austen or Dickens is being offered in the cinemas. Let the schedulers, Richard and Judy or Oprah do our choosing for us. Even Jonathan Franzen, author of *The Corrections* (2001), after an initial perfunctory rebellion, had to bow the neck to her in order that she choose his book. Had he not, his publishers would have committed hara-kiri. Lionel Trilling should have been so lucky.[2]

Choice, if it exists, will be pseudo choice – as between a Big Mac, a Quarter Pounder, a Whopper and a Wendyburger. The dilemma which is no dilemma is parodied in the wry prelude to Quentin Tarantino's 1994 film *Pulp Fiction*, in which the hitmen Vince and Jules (played by Samuel L. Jackson and John Travolta) are on their way to a job. Vince has just come back from Holland, superintending the Dutch drug connection:

Peas in a Pod: Jules and Vince

VINCENT You know what the funniest thing about Europe is?

JULES What?

VINCENT It's the little differences. A lotta the same shit we got here they got there, but there they're a little different.

JULES Examples?

VINCENT Well, in Amsterdam, you can buy beer in a movie theater. And I don't mean in a paper cup either. They give you a glass of beer, like in a bar. In Paris, you can buy beer at McDonald's. Also, you know what they call a Quarter Pounder with Cheese in Paris?

JULES They don't call it a Quarter Pounder with Cheese?

VINCENT No, they got the metric system there, they wouldn't know what the fuck a Quarter Pounder is.

JULES What'd they call it?

VINCENT *Royale* with Cheese.

JULES (repeating) *Royale* with Cheese. What'd they call a Big Mac?

VINCENT Big Mac's a Big Mac, but they call it *Le Big Mac*.

JULES What do they call a Whopper?

VINCENT I dunno, I didn't go into a Burger King.

Pulp fiction (low-level 'genre' fiction) is itself, of course, a matter of pseudo choice. That's Tarantino's joke. There are, as I write, five Frank Miller 'Sin City' titles on the graphic fiction top fifty bestseller list, all of them riding on the coattails of the 2005 movie, which Miller co-directed with Robert Rodriguez: Sin City: *The Hard Goodbye; Sin City: Booze, Broad and Bullets; Sin City: The Big Fat Kill; Sin City: The Yellow Bastard; Sin City: Family Values.* What's it to be? Quarter Pounder, Big Mac or Whopper? Same difference. I have seen the future of the Anglo-American book trade. It has golden arches. Big M, Big W same difference.

There has, however, been some encouraging readers' resistance to this. Most encouraging is the spread of reading clubs, in which people get together, effectively, to vote on what they will read together. During storms, cattle huddle together for protection. Under the book avalanche, readers clearly follow the same protective herding strategy.

But cattle also stampede under stress (cowboys, as I recall from the 1948 movie *Red River*, would sing their herds lullabies at night, like so many colicky babies). How else to explain the events of 16 July 2005, when the sixth instalment of J. K.

Rowling's superselling Potter saga was released on the stroke
of midnight? Excitement about *Harry Potter and the Half-Blood
Prince* had been stoked up to the pitch of nationwide hysteria.
The books themselves were guarded with for-your-eyes-
only secrecy. The government's contingency plans for sneak
attack by Saddam's weapons of mass destruction could not
have been more secure. Bloomsbury, Rowling's publishers,
must presumably have employed deaf and dumb printers.
Tantalising hints were thrown out, for weeks beforehand,
about the 'secret' the new volume would contain – the death
of a main character. But whose would it be? Voldemort (yes!)?
Professor Dumbledore (no!)? Hermione (please, God, no!)

No review copies were distributed – who needed good
notices? The books were bonded like contraband in the ware-
houses, until the countdown to HP hour. As it approached,
crowds gathered in high streets throughout the country.
Many were decked out in pointed hats with broomsticks and
the accoutrements of witchcraft and wizardry (as, wretch-
edly, were many of the shop assistants kept from their beds
by Pottermania). Covens were convoked outside bookshops.
Possibly goats were slaughtered in the alleys behind: anything
was possible. As the witching hour – midnight – neared, the
queues seethed. When the doors opened, it was a buying
stampede. Readers were no more *selecting* Rowling's book
from the thousands available elsewhere in the store than a
crowd, in a burning cinema, would pause to buy popcorn on
their rush to the exit. Follow the thundering herd was the
order of the night. Over a million copies of *Harry Potter and
the Half-Blood Prince* were sold over the counters in the United
Kingdom in twenty-four hours and as many by the electronic
bookstores. It was less selling than biblio-carpet bombing.

There is no point in lamenting the book world that history

has landed us with – a world in which millions of books are dumped in the market place at once, where over 10,000 newly published novels are on offer every year (and ten times that many available in the backlist). Whatever else, book glut is surely better than book famine. The problem is how to handle that glut – either by ruthless thinning out, or by new ways of organising the mass. Gluttony itself no longer suffices to clear a way through it. How can we get to the point where we can use fiction for whichever of the infinitely many uses we have for it and not be crushed by its sheer commercial and cultural weight?

I have organised what follows as a kind of zoom shot: first contemplating the book (specifically the novel) as an astronomer might a distant object in space; then moving the camera ('genre', 'the fiction industry') until, eventually close up, I target first the volume, then the page, then the words on the page. What began with something analogous to a stargazer regarding space through his telescope ends as something more like a biologist examining a specimen through a microscope.

Two more humble assumptions are constant: 1) novels are things to be enjoyed; 2) the better we read them, the more enjoyment we will derive from them. A clever engagement with a novel is, in my opinion, one of the more noble functions of human intelligence. Reading novels is not a spectator sport but a participatory activity. Done well, a good reading is as creditable as a 10-scoring high dive. It is, I would maintain, almost as difficult to read a novel well as to write one well. Which is greater, Henry James the critic or Henry James the novelist? Few of us can aspire to read as well as the Master – but then, even fewer can write fiction as well. No one, arguably.[3]

In terms of the politics of reading novels (if that is not too pompous an idea) I believe strongly what Orwell said – that books make society better insofar as their effect is to raise, or depress, all other cultural activities. If you want to know the overall health of a society, look at the quality of the books it is currently consuming. As Orwell put it, in the darkest days of the Blitz, in 1942:

> [T]he average book which the ordinary man reads is a better book than it would have been three years ago. One phenomenon of the war has been the enormous sale of Penguin Books, Pelican Books and other cheap titles, most of which would have been regarded as impossibly highbrow a few years back. And this in turn reacts on the newspapers, making them more serious and less sensational than they were before. It probably reacts also on the radio, and will react in time on the cinema.

All the boats go up with the book.

chapter 2

Declarations of independence

The only advice, indeed, that one person can give
another about reading, is to take no advice, to follow
your own instincts, to use your own reason, to come to
your own conclusions.

Virginia Woolf, 'How One Should Read a Book' (1926)

IF COMPUTER TYPESETTING were to allow it – and it
probably does – Woolf's testy instruction (don't ask *me* how
to read a novel, I merely write the things) should be cast, glim-
mering in neon red, over every page of what follows. Rather
like the Cretan liar of myth (everything I say is a lie, including
this), Woolf – one of whose more remunerative sidelines
was telling people, very firmly, how they should read books
– offers no advice other than ignore all advice including her
own. Follow your gut 'instinct'. Go alone into the world of
fiction.[4]

But, considered carefully, Woolf, subtle as ever, is not
endorsing the philistine colonel's bluff motto, 'I don't know

much about literature, but I know what I like – and so does my wife.' 'Coming to your own conclusions', with every resource of mind, intellect and sensibility, is less an act of judgement than one of self-definition. And difficult. In reading a good novel well we can discover something about ourselves – more specifically, how different we, as individuals, are from each of the other five-and-a-half billion individuals on the planet. A novel is, or can be, a kind of Rorschach Test – a reflection of us, in all our private complexities, in one of the better mirrors that contemporary life can hold up to us.

Some of these differences and complexities are built into our hard wiring – aspects of ourselves which we can no more change than we can add a cubit to our height. To illustrate the point, consider one of the certifiably great novels of our time, Toni Morrison's *Beloved* (1987) – a text which, following the author's Nobel award in 1993, has become as widely studied in American high schools and college Lit-101 courses as *Hamlet*.

Morrison's novel is, crudely speaking, *Uncle Tom's Cabin* recycled from a post-1960s standpoint politically and racially, and a post-modernist standpoint aesthetically. *Beloved*'s narrative chronicles the experiences of Sethe, a former slave, and her post-traumatic recovery a decade after emancipation. The novel needs no explication from me – it is a much exegetised text. But consider, for a moment, the book's cryptic epigraph, at the head of the narrative:

Sixty Million
and more

It is a tendentious statistic. And it is almost certainly inaccurate. The number of Africans estimated to have perished on the 'middle passage' to the New World or in slavery there has ranged as high as 120 million and as low (if that is the right word) as a tenth of that amount. No one, shamefully, will ever know precisely, because no one at the time cared so long as the black cargo made money for its traders. No one counted heads any more than the Peruvian fisherman counts sardines in his net.

Morrison quite clearly chose sixty million as a multiple of six million. That, famously, is the rounded estimate of the number of European Jews who died in the Holocaust. What point, then, is Toni Morrison making? Something akin, I suspect, to Linda Loman's agonised lament in Arthur Miller's *Death of a Salesman*: 'Attention must be finally paid!'

Finally is a long time coming. America, which is commendably sensitive to the horrors of the Jewish genocide, has, Morrison suggests, been conveniently amnesiac about the genocidal crime, ten times more criminal, on which the Founding Fathers' republic complacently rests. *Beloved* is a narrative about repressed memory, which manifests itself as a ghost, coming back to haunt the forgetful. The forgetting is both personal (Sethe buries the memory of having murdered her child) and collective (America buries the memory of slavery – or veneers it with glossy *Gone with the Wind* romanticism). Some things must not be forgotten, the novel asserts. Attention must be finally paid.

In terms of where they start from, an American Jew and an African American may well read 'Sixty Million and more' differently, and the flavour thrown over *Beloved*'s narrative by its epigraph may provoke quite different kinds of resentment. A Jewish reader may think that Morrison is somehow diminishing the Second World War horror (mine is bigger than yours). An African American may feel that their own tragic history has been marginalised by the attention generated by what critics have (unfairly) called the Holocaust industry.

None the less, both kinds of reader, when they embark on the novel, can rise above any partisan ethnic resentment. What the critic I. A. Richards called 'fictional belief' comes into play. One falls back on the wonderful elasticity of sensibility by which, for example, a Protestant can be sympathetically moved by Gerard Manley Hopkins's ultra-Catholic 'terrible sonnets', a gentile reader can respond to Bernard Malamud's *The Fixer* (1966) – or a male reader can fully identify with the suffering of Morrison's Sethe when she is sexually violated, in the most vile way, by 'Schoolteacher's' nephews. As George Eliot argued, modern society has no better generator of intelligent sympathy than the novel, and no more efficient dissipater of prejudice.

But even elastic will break if it is stretched too far. I doubt whether any Jewish American, or African American, could overcome their gag reflex disgust at William L. Pierce's *The Turner Diaries* – the 1978 novel which the FBI, not normally known for its lit crit expertise, has labelled the 'bible of the extreme right'. Pierce's neo-Nazi *tendenzroman* fantasises a wholesale slaughter of every American of colour and the cleansing nuclear destruction by 'Aryan Americans' of the 'two Jew capitals' – Tel Aviv and New York. Notoriously, the Oklahoma bomber Timothy McVeigh, along with likeminded domestic terrorists, found inspiration and instruction in *The Turner Diaries* and in its 1984 sequel of racist vigilantism (ethnic cleansing by the assassin's gun), *Hunter*. Even if Pierce wrote with the skill of Proust and the verve of Tom Clancy – which he does not – few, other than his co-extremists, could relish his fiction. The mass of readers are hard-wired to reject it.

There are, however, trickier examples than Pierce's

obscene tracts. Leon Uris, a post-war bestseller, has rarely
been thought of as a 'literary' novelist. Yet he was, as the semi-
autobiographical *Battle Cry* (1953) (the fifth best American
Second World War novel, by my reckoning)[5] attests, a workmanlike practitioner. Uris's 1976 docu-historical romance
Trinity (sub James Michener), about Ireland and the Fenian
movement, was, however, raised to the level of a sacred text by
the post-1969 Provisional IRA. The novel was a consolation to
the hunger striker Bobby Sands, in his self-martyrising star-
vation, in British captivity. As one jaundiced commentator
recalled, he added to the suffering of his fellow internees by
insisting on reading it aloud to them. Bad novels – or, in Uris's
case, less than great novels – can inspire historic acts.[6]

Politics (including sexual politics) can do odd things to
one's perception of fiction and one's judgements of it. Visiting
an Ivy League college in 2001, I saw displayed on a noticeboard
the announcement of a women's reading group meeting
summoned to discuss J. M. Coetzee's *Disgrace* (1999). It was,
the notice succinctly declared by way of synopsis, 'the story
of a professor who seduces his women students'. Lecturer's
lechery is undeniably an element in Coetzee's plot. David Lurie
– a bleakly lonely, twice divorced man – indifferently slakes
his pleasureless lusts with prostitutes, departmental secre-
taries and students. He is a glum, affectless, incorrigible serial
shagger. The tone of the book may be taken from the description of his seduction (date rape?) of Melanie, who has been
excited by his course on Wordsworth. He, on his part, has been
excited, rather more carnally, by watching Melanie rehearse for
a student dramatic production. The hunter makes his move:

At four o'clock the next afternoon he is at her flat. She
opens the door wearing a crumpled T-shirt, cycling

shorts, slippers in the shape of comic-book gophers which he finds silly, tasteless.

He has given her no warning; she is too surprised to resist the intruder who thrusts himself upon her. When he takes her in his arms, her limbs crumple like a marionette's. Words heavy as clubs thud into the delicate whorl of her ear. 'No, not now!' she says, struggling. 'My cousin will come back.'

But nothing will stop him. He carries her to the bedroom, brushes off the absurd slippers, kisses her feet, astonished by the feeling she evokes. Something to do with the apparition on the stage: the wig, the wiggling bottom, the crude talk. Strange love! Yet from the quiver of Aphrodite, goddess of the foaming waves, no doubt about that.

She does not resist. All she does is avert herself; avert her lips, avert her eyes. She lets him lay her out on the bed and undress her: she even helps him, raising her arms and then her hips. Little shivers of cold run through her; as soon as she is bare, she slips under the quilted counterpane like a mole burrowing and turns her back on him.

Not rape, not quite that, but undesired nevertheless, undesired to the core. As though she had decided to go slack, die within herself for the duration, like a rabbit when the jaws of the fox close on its neck. So that everything done to her might be done, as it were, far away.

'Pauline will be back any minute,' she says when it is over. 'Please. You must go.'

He obeys, but then, when he reaches his car, is overtaken with such dejection, such dullness, that he sits slumped at the wheel unable to move.

A mistake, a huge mistake.

It is worse than a mistake. It is disgracefully wrong. But it is, as Coetzee presents it, far from simple wrongdoing. The point of the novel, as I read it – but as I doubt the women's group did – is less Lurie's predatory sexual habits than his stiff-necked obstinacy, as a white South African, when confronted with his offences and offered 'sensitivity training' and rehabilitation. His employers are understanding. Lurie declines the offer gracelessly. He accepts, nay embraces, 'disgrace'.

Lurie's obstinate determination not to be forgiven is paralleled in the second half of the novel when his daughter, who has been gang-raped by a band of marauding Africans, obstinately refuses to report the crime to the police – even after discovering the identity of one of her assailants. It is a post-apartheid South African thing and reflects, enigmatically, on Truth and Reconciliation tribunals. Such operations are harder, the novel seems to say, than the political optimists claim. The disgrace of apartheid runs too deep. Reparation and suffering, not kiss and make up, are what are needed.

It was such explorations of the human complexity that lies behind political change which induced the Nobel committee in 2003 to elevate Coetzee as a laureate alongside Morrison. The grey men of Stockholm like fiction which takes on big themes – so long, as was with the case of Graham Greene's *England Made Me* (1935), they happen *not* to be big themes that reflect badly on Stockholm. Greene's 'entertainment', as he called it, about Sweden's Robert Maxwell, the 'match king' Ivar Kreuger, ensured its author a one-way ticket to the Nobel black list. Pearl S. Buck, author of the plodding Chinese epic *The Good Earth* (1931), committed no such offence, and duly got her Swedish prize in 1938.

I, as a university professor, teaching, as it happens, the same subjects as Lurie, will necessarily read the above quoted passage from *Disgrace* differently from a woman undergraduate. How can I not? How can she not? It's in our wiring. A South African professor would, I think, read it differently from a Swedish colleague – and, of course, the grey men who awarded Coetzee the Nobel. Black men will read *Disgrace* differently from grey (or white) men, and all of them differently from women. But all readers can, I think, converge constructively on the moral complexities which Coetzee explores, with the uniquely delicate instrumentality that the novel makes available to those practitioners with the skills to use it.

To label *Disgrace* 'the story of a professor who seduces his students' is as blinkered an interpretation as to say the novel is 'the story of an innocent white girl who is brutally gang-raped by black thugs' – a notice which would not, I suspect, have survived long on the noticeboard of an Ivy League university. Or to label *Beloved* 'the story of an innocent black slave who is brutally sodomised by her white overseers'. That might survive on the noticeboard, but it would be a travesty. You cannot simplify such novels in this way. As D. H. Lawrence put it, 'If you try to nail anything down in the novel you either kill the novel, or the novel gets up and walks away with the nail.' None the less, self-evidently, we are incorrigibly prone to pulling all sorts of nails out of the fiction we read.

Axiomatically, a good reader (or 'user') of good fiction will read (use) the same novel in a uniquely different way from every other good reader – and, potentially, just as well. If you can be bothered to work it out, there is only one correct solution to the mathematical problem: 'If an orange costs five-sixths of the price of an apple and an apple costs 27p, how much would a packet of six oranges cost, to the nearest penny?'[7]

There are, by contrast, as many correct ways of reading *Oranges are Not the Only Fruit* as there are competent readers of Jeanette Winterson's 1985 novel. I once wrote to the author to ask whether in the novel the heroine Jeanette's mother was gay. I received a postcard, decorated charmingly with oranges, by return with the simple question, 'Who knows, John?' The implication being 'Work it out for yourself' (as it happens, I think the answer to my question is 'yes' – but who knows, John?). I would have received the same answer had I asked whether the Jeanette in the novel is Jeanette the novelist. Work it out for yourself.

The freedom of the reader to read, and thereby 'own' the novel, is defiantly expressed by Paul Auster in his 1995 collection of stories *The Red Notebook*: 'The one thing I try to do in all my books is to leave enough room in the prose for the reader to inhabit it. Because I finally believe it's the reader who writes the book and not the writer.' Few novelists, I suspect, would surrender their authorial sovereignty as entirely as Auster suggests (nor, I suspect, would Paul Auster in the face of gross misreadings of his novels). But his paradox – it is the reader who writes – expresses a basic truth about what goes on when you are reading fiction. Two-way streets which, ideally, meet up (but, regrettably, sometimes do not).

I cannot, as Woolf instructs us, prescribe or predict 'conclusions' for others where novels are concerned. I can, however, suggest ways of getting there. But then, probably, it will be one of those Johnsonian conclusions 'in which nothing is concluded' – the title of the last section in 'the Great Cham of Literature's' sole venture into fiction, *Rasselas* (1759). One may also note that he wrote the novel in two weeks to pay for his mother's funeral. Never forget that novelists, most of them, have to pay their bills like the rest of us and craft their work accordingly. Or, as Brecht put it, 'Erst fressen' – 'Grub comes first'.

Predictably, the harder conclusions are worked at, the more different the results will be. To illustrate the point, consider the well-publicised act of collective reading which goes into the judging of the annual award of the Man Booker Prize. The regulations decree one deceptively simple criterion. The judges shall, in their wisdom, identify 'the best novel of the year' first published in the United Kingdom, in English, by an author who can claim nationality in that territory which, in Britain's century (the nineteenth), was coloured red on the world map. The Empire, in short. The winner is guaranteed fame, wealth – but not, as we shall see, unanimous critical approval.

Five Man Booker judges are appointed annually. They are presumed to be competent readers of fiction and are expected to be diligent in the discharge of their judicial duties. Around 120 titles are submitted for judgement, to be whittled down into a long list, a shortlist and, finally, the last novel standing, like Russell Crowe, over the steaming carcasses of its defeated rivals.

There is another, less public combat involved in the award. It has never happened in the thirty-six years since it was launched, according to the long-term administrator of the Prize, Martyn Goff, that the five judges have gone into their conclusive meeting in harmonious agreement about their verdicts. The year 2005 was no exception. Each of the judges had a different favourite when they entered their final enclave. The winner was a shortlist title wholly unfavoured by the bookies, who gave it odds of 7–1, The Sea by John Banville. The novel is, to quote myself as chairman of the judges, 'a study of alcoholism, melancholy, terminal disease, family disintegration, the decay of age. Permeated with slit-your-throat gloom,

The Sea does not contribute to the cheeriness of life. But neither does life, if you've lived enough of it.' It is, however, exquisitely written – or, some objected, overwritten.

'Surprising' was the most common epithet to describe our verdict in the morning's papers. Divisive-down-the-middle would have been more accurate. For one Fleet Street literary editor, Boyd Tonkin of the *Independent*, the choice of Banville threatened not merely the future of the Man Booker Prize, but literature itself. James's venerable House of Fiction (as he liked to allegorise the English novel) had been shaken to its very foundation by the Man Booker judges' signal act of cultural perversion. It was – Tonkin's language was not minced – a 'disaster':

> Yesterday the Man Booker judges made possibly the worst, certainly the most perverse, and perhaps the most indefensible choice in the 36-year history of the contest. By choosing John Banville's *The Sea*, they selected an icy and over-controlled exercise in coterie aestheticism ahead of a shortlist, and a long list, packed with a plenitude of riches and delights.
>
> The Dublin novelist, whose emotional range is limited and whose prose exhibits all the chilly perfection of a waxwork model, must today count himself as the luckiest writer on the planet. This was a travesty of a result from a travesty of a judging process.

Perplexingly, four months earlier, when *The Sea* was published, the paper had published reviews, commissioned by same editor, asserting precisely the opposite judgement. Banville, the *Independent's* reviewer Peter J. Conradi asserted, 'is prodigiously gifted ... Everything in Banville's books is alive. Bleakly elegant, he is a writer's writer, a new Henry

Green.' And, in the *Independent on Sunday* John Tague was even more laudatory: 'The Sea confirms Banville's reputation as one of the finest prose stylists working in English today and, in the sheer beauty of its achievement, is unlikely to be bettered by any other novel published this year.' The Booker judges, after their ritual disagreements, agreed.

How can a novel, examined so dutifully and on so many fronts, be judged at the same time as utterly bad and outstandingly good? The same rave-plus-hatchet job was repeated a few weeks later, when *The Sea* was published in America. Then, in the annual round-up of books of the year, in December 2005, the fiction editor of the *Sunday Times* declared *The Sea* to be a disgraceful choice, which had brought the prize to a 'low ebb' (sea ... ebb – get it?) The literary editor of the *Observer*, on the same Sunday, made it one of the handful of the very best books of the year. Perplexing.

Only in Ireland was the award to one of its own given unmitigated approval. The Taoiseach himself, Bertie Ahern, sent Banville official congratulations. Would Tony Blair, I wonder, have phoned Zadie Smith had she won? In his native country Banville is regarded as a fit successor to Beckett and Joyce. There were dark aspersions against the London literary world's incorrigible 'bitchery', and suspicions were voiced as to why, in the thirty-six years of the prize's history – it began in 1969, simultaneously with the Troubles in Ulster – only two sons of Ireland had won (the other being Roddy Doyle). Why, for example, did Tonkin label Banville 'the Dublin novelist'? Would Salman Rushdie have been 'the Bombay novelist', Coetzee the 'Adelaide novelist', or Kazuo Ishiguro 'the Nagasaki novelist'? What had birthplace or place of residence to do with it? It was not quite the Ayatollah and Salman – but there was a distinct sense that national hackles had been raised by the Banville affair. Fiction, it would seem, can still get people's blood up. And sometimes, as *The Satanic Verses* (1988) demonstrated, spill it.

Regarding the hoo-hah his novel had provoked, Banville, in his sardonic way, observed that 'if so many people are angry, I must be doing something right'. At last, his publishers must have muttered. An author whose name could previously barely sell 4000 a title cleared 75,000 in a fortnight post-Booker and figured in the UK and US bestseller lists for the rest of the year. *The Sea* was floating on a high tide. At the very least, John Banville now has the chance to write his name large in annals of literature. Whether he succeeds, only time will tell.

This hammer and tongs is repeated, year in year out. It is galling that, in order to induce people to buy, read and get enthused by good fiction, one needs a to-the-death contest with one novel left standing and so many good novels left by the way. And it is odd that experts who presume to pronounce on literature for a living can never seem to get their act together. The harder they set themselves to the task, the more eloquently and passionately divergent their opinions are. Why, when it comes to fiction, cannot we get along? Why this genteel critical riot?

The outcome of the Man Booker prize looks chaotic but, in truth, it is simply a playing out, on a national stage, of what happens every day where novels are read. And, for all the confusion, ding-dong and spurting of bad blood, it is healthy – the democracy of mature critical sensibility. Virginia Woolf was right – there is no consensus; no right way to read, no 'correct' reading of any good novel. Bad novels, however, are something else; we can despise William L. Pierce in unison – but even he has his corps of skinheaded admirers for whom spitting probably comes easier than literary criticism.

chapter 3

Every other thing has changed: why hasn't the book changed?

A MINDGAME. Put William Caxton in H. G. Wells's time machine and transport him from his busy little stall by Westminster Abbey, AD 1480, to Oxford Street, London, or Fifth Avenue, New York, summer 2006.

The founder of our British book trade would, like the philosopher William James's newborn babe, find himself in a booming, buzzing mass of confusion. Everything would seem as strange as Mr Wells's chronomobile which transported him here. What are these self-propelled carts, purring, coughing, belching fumes and irascibly honking? Why are the pedestrians holding what look like prayer books to their ears and murmuring into them? Breviaries?

The profusion of female limbs and, in summer, more than limbs, might disturb medieval proprieties. In the windows (so much glass!) are what look like – can it be? – sorcerers' crystals? Screens on which images flicker and shift. Music, very strange music, thunders out from the mouth of the shops: but no jongleur or troubadour can be seen. Devilry. Everywhere.

One thing, however, would be comfortingly familiar to the master printer: the contents of Waterstone's, Borders and Barnes & Noble. Master Caxton might not understand how Mr Wells's time machine, or any other machine, worked. But he would know (roughly) how the Penguin Classic edition of H. G. Wells's *The Time Machine* had been manufactured.

The physical book, the master printer would have been overjoyed to discover, had changed hardly a jot. He would even have found his own catalogue leader, Chaucer's *Canterbury Tales* (c. 1380s–90s), in the Classics section. Some physical aspects of the books on display would strike him as nifty improvements on the fifteenth-century commodity: dustjackets, indexes, covers (he, of course, sold his wares from his Westminster stall in quires), coated paper, italic print, perfect binding – all worth sticking in the boot of Mr Wells's wonderful machine for the trip back. But despite all these peripheral improvements to the book as a book, Master Caxton, or his apprentices, Wynkyn de Worde and Richard Pynson, could, with their fifteenth-century technology, mock up the same product that the big W is currently pushing on its '3 for 2' tables.

Why has the codex book endured so unchangingly? Why is its basic form, apparently, beyond improvement? Forget Wells. In my own lifetime, the shellac 78 rpm ten-inch record, designed for the wind-up steel needle and acoustic gramophone, has been replaced by the albumed vinyl LP (beautiful objects, I miss them), the CD and, most recently, the iPod stashed with up to 15,000 tracks. Head implants, doubtless, are on the way, for the dedicated music lover. Seattle is working on it.

Over the same period, shellac-to-silicon, my Penguin paperbacks have remained what they always were. If one brought Allen Lane, founder of Penguin Books, forward on the time machine from 1935, nothing much about his company's books AD 2006 would look different to him – except, perhaps, the ubiquitous pictorial covers; something he loathed and laboured ceaselessly to put down. What would really cheese off Lane – 'King Penguin' – would be the fact that his imprint, which did so much for British culture, was no longer king of the bookshop, as it had been in its post-war heyday.

The codex book (that is, cut pages clapped together sequentially between covers), bibliographers instruct us, long precedes the fifteenth-century introduction of printing from Germany. Those who first saw Gutenberg's or Caxton's products viewed the things with no great excitement as a new, and not very surprising kind of manuscript. Gutenberg's Bible doesn't even look like print to the modern eye. Codex packaged manuscripts had been around for a millennium before Gutenberg. Moveable type simply made such familiar objects easier to produce, or imprint, in mass; as did the steam press and stereotyping in the early nineteenth century and computer typesetting in the 1970s. Print merely mechanised the scriptorium as, 400 years later, the silicon chip was to automate the print shop.

The medieval book trade received its greatest boost not from hot-lead type but from the manufacture of rag and grass-based papers. Paper was a Chinese invention which had also been around for centuries before European printers discovered it. Its arrival was a relief to the animal population of Europe, whose livestock had been disembowelled by the thousand for vellum. Moveable type and paper converged with the massed literacy and penmanship generated by the monasteries to produce print culture, and the efficient storage, ordering, transmission and circulation of information which has made the modern world possible. Print culture is, in turn, the foundation of the only major literary form whose origins we can confidently place in historical time: the novel. Literally a 'new thing'.

The third century AD Emperor Heliogabalus reportedly offered a prize for anyone who could come up with a new vice. The Roman orgy had it seems, become boring. An improved version of the codex seems similarly beyond human ingenuity. But the whitecoats at MIT are busily working on electronic paper and futuristic 'books'. The following bulletin (dated 2005) on the website of Drs Joseph M. Jacobson, Barrett Comiskey, Patrick Anderson and Leila Hasan records that

> Books with printed pages are unique in that they embody the simultaneous, high-resolution display of hundreds of pages of information. The representation of information on a large number of physical pages, which may be physically turned and written on, constitutes a highly preferred means of information interaction. An obvious disadvantage of the printed page, however, is its immutability once typeset. We are currently developing electronically addressable paper-page displays that use real paper substrates. This effort includes the development of novel electronically addressable contrast media, microencapsulation chemistry, and desktop printing technologies to print functional circuits, logic, and display elements on paper or paper-like substrates, including interconnecting vias and multi-layer logic.[8]

Exciting stuff – assuming one can understand it ('vias'?) But what emerges from the lab as 'e-paper' and 'e-ink' (another MIT wheeze that was all the rage at the January 2006

Consumers Electronic Show) will, I suspect, have the same relationship to the real thing that the blow-up sex doll has to [fill in your preferred, or wished for, partner here]. Something vital will be missing.

The future of fiction is in your hand

Technology keeps chipping away at the book, rather like the bird which, by removing a grain of sand every thousand years, will eventually flatten the mountain. One of the more interesting innovations in 2005 was the commercial downloading of audio books into the vast storage capacity of the iPod. Although Apple's device is primarily intended for archiving, accessioning and replaying music, the 60 gigabyte version can serve just as well to play back *War and Peace* and about a hundred other full-length novels. The ideal single luxury for your desert island. Or, if you stick to music, it offers some 14,992 more tracks than Roy Plomley's miserly eight.

iPodded audio fiction is much more convenient than the clunky tapes with which the audiobook form emerged commercially two decades ago, or the CD format which eventually replaced the tape. iPod fiction also has the commercial advantage of P2P – publishers can supply directly to the consumer, without the intervention of the middleman (that is, bookseller), which is very much a wave of the future.

The future arrives faster nowadays. In December 2005, iCue launched their successor to Gutenberg – downloadable novels, in text form, via the mobile phone. The handy iCue would, its maker prophesied, do for fiction what the iPod had done for popular music, and what the codex had done for the papyrus scroll. It was the next big thing.

For a modest charge, around £2 a text, you can buy a

work of fiction (the first was, seasonally enough, Dickens's *A Christmas Carol* (1843)). Tucked away in the mobile's capacious memory the novel can then be played on the phone's tiny screen in one of three flexible formats: 'page', 'ticker' and 'flicker'. 'Page' supplies the reader with a quad-rilateral layout of about eighty formatted words – depending on the font and point size chosen. The miniaturised folio is rather too much for an eyebite, but too little for the digestion of context which the standard 400-word page (800-word double page spread) allows – flicking back, for example, around the page to ascertain how things hold together. 'Ticker' runs the text across the screen like ticker tape, or the 'crawl line' on rolling news programmes. Speed can be adjusted. The 'flicker' option shoots single words at the reader's eye, in a range of speeds from snail to machine gun. How, I wonder, would the Blackberry screen handle a mobile-centric novel such as Lucy Kellaway's 2005 satire on twenty-first century office life, *Martin Lukes: Who Moved My Blackberry?*, the narrative of which is conducted entirely in modish email epistolary form?

iCue is yet another ingenious attempt at Mark Twain's better mousetrap. Invent such a device, Twain said, and the world will beat a path to your door. One has not, alas, been deafened by the sound of thundering feet to iCue's electronic portal. The book does not seem imperilled (nor, oddly, is the cheese-and-spring-loaded mousetrap).

iCue has the undoubted advantage that it is lean-back, unlike the lean-forward computer VDU – a device which has probably done as much damage to the human spine as the keyboard has to humanity's carpal tunnel. The iCue can be used in an easy chair, unlike the computer monitor – or even the misnamed laptop, which should really be called the 'knee balancer'. Imagine being stuck on a train in a tunnel (likely enough in the UK in 2005), passing the time with your iCue and some distracting work of fiction – although, if you had thought ahead, a book picked up at the station bookstore would be more welcome, if less pocket-portable.

Even though the makers claim that readers can habituate themselves to the iCue experience in three minutes, the format feels uncomfortable. At full rat-a-tat speed, for example, the 'flicker' option is dizzying. And until hologram enlargement is perfected, creating a conventional octavo-sized surface, the mobile screen is too cramped for comfort. Like the Victorian trick of inscribing the Lord's Prayer on the back of a penny-post stamp (one of Thackeray's party pieces), just because it is amazing does not mean you particularly want to strain your eyes reading it.

And, as has been demonstrated time and time again in the laboratory, words pixel-created on a grey screen (even the largest words and smallest pixels) are marginally harder work for the human eye to decode than words ink-inscribed on a page (hence why this book, like most other books, has been edited on old-fashioned paper). It is the difference between swimming in water and swimming in treacle. For short messages (email, texting, for example) it does not matter. When you have a quarter of a million words of Moby-Dick to take on board, it matters.

It may all be a matter of technological transitionality. Possibly VDU legibility will take a quantum leap forwards in the near future and that scientific mirage, 'electronic paper', will become reality. It may also be a generational thing. Young eyes versus old eyes. Teenagers, it was reported in 2005, increasingly request that – should the worst happen – they be buried with their mobiles in their hand (Edgar Allan Poe

could have used that idea). The phone is as much a part of
them as Ahab's whalebone leg was part of him.

For those whose eyes and thumbs have grown up with
the ever-mutating mobile phone, the iCued *Moby-Dick* may
well seem as natural an object as an apple growing on a tree.
Time will tell. My guess, though, is that, should Caxton make
another trip in fifty years time, there will still be a lot which,
as a master printer, he would recognise. And there will still be
bookstores to recognise it in.

What are the features of the codex which have enabled it
to survive so long? It is, as I have previously said, a lean-
back, not a lean-forward apparatus – and human beings
like nothing more than to relax while they read, or spectate.
Armchairs and VDUs are not natural partners. The codex,
unlike the scroll or the clay tablet, is wonderfully portable.
'Pocket book' is a much more accurate term than 'palm
pilot' or 'laptop'. In authoritarian regimes, for whom books
have always represented danger, the codex could be usefully
secreted about the person. One attractive theory is that the
codex revolution began with Bibles, concealed under robes,
by early Christians in pagan Rome. The French Revolution,
as book historians such as Robert Darnton have argued,[9] was
fuelled by *philosophe* tracts, easily smuggled in from across
the Swiss border (including Voltaire's revolutionary 1759
novel, *Candide*). In Soviet Russia, resistance was mobilised
by handmade codices – the so-called samizdats (including
Solzhenitsyn's incendiary novels). Meanwhile, the Soviet
authorities waged ceaseless war against Mormons, and other
evangelical sects, smuggling Bibles – God's novel – into the
godless territory behind the Iron Curtain. The CIA actually
sponsored the dropping, by covert overflights, of copies of

Orwell's 1945 novel-cum-fantasia *Animal Farm*, translated into the captive peoples' local tongue.

Books are what the Victorians called 'edge tools' and are therefore – like knives and other weaponry – habitually subject to state control. Few literary forms have been as censored, historically, as the novel. More significant is the fact that reading, done well, is, as I said in Chapter 2, an act of self-definition. Put another way, it is a solitary vice. One reads, as one dreams, defecates and masturbates – alone.

Police understand the self-defining aspect of fiction. They take a keen interest in a suspect's bookshelves. The 'Unabomber', Theodore Kaczynski, loved Joseph Conrad's *The Secret Agent* (1907) and had read the book over a dozen times. Yigal Amir, the murderer of Yitzhak Rabin, had Frederick Forsyth's 1971 thriller about a professional assassin *The Day of the Jackal* on his shelf – pages dealing with public assassination strategically marked. Timothy McVeigh, as he made his escape from the devastated Murrah Building in Oklahoma City, had a sheaf of xeroxed pages from *The Turner Diaries* under his arm. Tom Sneddon, the Santa Maria DA, obtained a court order to seize singer Michael Jackson's reading (and viewing) matter – and made prominent use of it in court. Our reading preferences are when carefully examined, as uniquely different, and as revealing, as our fingerprints.

Big Brother always wants to know, among everything else, what you are reading. The FBI's freedom to examine library records was one of the more obnoxious aspects of the 2001 PATRIOT Act, which led to fierce resistance to its being extended by the American Congress in December 2005. Surveillance was one thing; snooping another. Elsewhere the snooping was more insidious. The American economist R. Preston McAfee suggested that hip bookbuyers should try logging into Amazon with your own identity and asking for a price on something. Then clear your cookies (so Amazon cannot access your personal information and purchasing history) and search again anonymously for the same item. Sometimes you will be quoted a different price, because when Amazon looks at your past spending pattern, and sees that you have not always gone for the lowest price, they will treat you as a poor searcher – a more inelastic customer – and make you a less attractive offer.

Every time you buy a book on Amazon, you are being profiled, and adding to your profile. Jeff Bezos, like the director of the FBI, knows that you are what you read.

The solitariness of the reading act is its defining feature. And nowhere more than with fiction (the book which, as Paul Auster says, the reader 'writes') are we more truly ourselves. It is vital, vital even perhaps for society itself, to protect the privacy and solitude of the reading act – as vital as the curtain in the voting booth. Orwell makes the point with the image of Winston Smith, rebelliously reading Emmanuel Goldstein's tract on collectivism in the corner of his Victory Mansions apartment, secluded as he fondly believes from the all-seeing telescreen, in *Nineteen Eighty-Four* (1949). The sinister machine (which we have come to love) is described in the novel's third chapter:

> Inside the flat a fruity voice was reading out a list of figures which had something to do with the production of pig iron. The voice came from an oblong metal plaque like a dulled mirror which formed part of the surface of the right-hand wall. Winston turned a switch and the voice sank somewhat, though the words were still distinguishable. The instrument (the telescreen, it was called)

could be dimmed, but there was no way of shutting it off completely.

The last sentence still rings true.

There was something dehumanising about the whole population of China reading Mao's *Little Red Book* publicly, simultaneously and in the same 'correct' way during the late 1960s. It was dehumanising in the same way as are the futuristic serfs in Fritz Lang's 1927 masterpiece *Metropolis*, who do everything, from walking, to eating, to copulating, to sleeping, en masse. Regimented reading is a contradiction in terms. And in the case of fiction, there is something faintly unsettling about the Da Vinci phenomenon. Did those twenty-five-million-and-rising punters freely *choose* to read the novel? Or were they merely drifting with some bestselling tide, as helpless as literate jellyfish to choose their course?

'Book' – *libre* (French), *liber* (Latin) – has to the ear inescapable overtones of 'liberty': personal freedom. The etymology is apparently false (the Latin originates in 'bark of a tree'). None the less, there is something intrinsically unchained, humanly 'free' in the reading act. One of the reassuring features of the current vogue for reading groups is the degree of disagreement they generate once the discussion gets going. Friends get together for the purpose of amicable quarrels. 'Is Heathcliff a swine or a tragic hero?': throw that question into the reading group and stand back. Chances are no two members of the group, however like-minded on other things, will entirely agree with each other at the beginning of the discussion, and – however opinions may have changed – members will usually disagree among themselves even more as the discussion (good naturedly) winds up.

The other notable feature of reading groups is how, unlike

the typical university seminar, they privilege the female voice. The earliest description I know of a reading group in fiction is in Jane Austen's *Northanger Abbey* (1818), where, learning of Catherine's enthusiasm for Mrs Radcliffe's 1794 gothic shocker *The Mysteries of Udolpho*, the bossy Isabella Thorpe, who has loaned her new friend her library copy, says:

> 'Dear creature! how much I am obliged to you; and when you have finished *Udolpho*, we will read the *Italian* together; and I have made out a list of twelve or more of the same kind for you.'

The young ladies, accompanied by Isabella's unimportant sisters, spend their mornings 'together' reading gothic novels, before the real business of the day in Bath – husband-hunting – begins. They can read a novel like Mrs Radcliffe's *The Italian* (1797) 'together' because Isabella will have taken out a multi-volume copy from one of the town's many circulating libraries. Volumes will shuffle between the ladies, with excited commentary and amiable disagreement.

Reading groups should, I sometimes feel, be called 'gossip groups'. Gossips (etymology: 'good sibs' or good sisters), a word which once was entirely approving in its overtones, were called in to a woman confined in pregnancy and childbirth to chat and take the mother-to-be's mind off her discomforts. Women have always been the best readers of fiction – which, typically, is what gossip is: 'stories' memorialising the events of the community, tittle-tattle, telling tales out of school. That does not mean, of course, that gossips will the best critics of fiction. But if you can read well, who needs critics?[10]

The book has survived innumerable death sentences. Not only has it survived, it has thrived. There is no reason to suppose that it will not continue to do so for a half century or more; perhaps for ever. One of the strange blindspots in science fiction is its pervasive vision of a future world that is bookless and fictionless – even though sf is itself, in origin, a book-based genre. Captain James T. Kirk, intrepid commander of the starship *Enterprise*, is no bookworm. As I recall from watching the series, his one reference to printed fiction is in the movie *Star Trek IV: The Voyage Home* (1986), where we discover that he and Spock have geared themselves for a trip back to the late twentieth century by dipping into the *oeuvres* of Jacqueline Susann and Harold Robbins. 'The giants', as Spock sagely observes. Let's hope the half-Vulcan is better on astral navigation.

What books survive in the starship *Enterprise*'s library are, it seems, a couple of tattered paperbacks – archaeological specimens. The one world into which they do not boldly go is the world of books. The future, it seems, can do without them. In *The Time Machine* (1898), there is a vivid scene in which Wells's traveller finds himself in the ruins of a public library, AD 802,701, and sees piles of 'brown and charred rags [which] I presently recognized as the decaying vestiges of books. They had long since dropped to pieces, and every semblance of print had left them. But here and there were warped boards and cracked metallic clasps that told the tale well enough.' Among that decayed debris are, presumably, the scientific romances of H. G. Wells. Orwell's *Nineteen Eighty-Four* forecasts a world where the only novels, as such, are churned out by the 'Pornosec', like so many sausages. In Ray Bradbury's *Fahrenheit 451* (written in the McCarthyite 1950s, but set in the 1990s), the state ruthlessly incinerates books and, in the woods, the rebels resist by converting themselves into human book sausages – 'I am *Weir of Hermiston*', etc.

The fact is, these dystopian forecasts of bookless, or book-degraded, worlds have traditionally missed the mark. There were magnitudes more books in 1984 than in 1948, and in 1994 than in 1984. No one reading this book in the early twenty-first century will, as with Orwell and Bradbury, be around to test the market in the ninth millennium but, the chances are the book will be in better shape than Wells foresaw. His traveller may have been bookless but look around the departure lounge at Heathrow or JFK and see the travellers, many of them, reading as intensely as trainee rabbis in a Jewish theological seminary.

The codex book still does things the computer cannot. Its IT superiority has been recognised by the father of British computing, Alan Turing. Computers, Turing observed, suffer from the same problem as Egyptian papyrus scrolls – you have to scroll through them to find what you want. The computer – or 'Turing Machine' – has the advantage over papyrus in that you can do it faster, but the process remains the same:

Digital computing machines [he wrote in February 1947] all have a central mechanism or control and some very extensive form of memory. The memory does not have to be infinite, but it certainly needs to be very large. In general the arrangement of the memory on an infinite tape is unsatisfactory in a practical machine, because of the large amount of time which is liable to be spent in shifting up and down the tape to reach the point at which a particular piece of information required at the moment is stored. Thus a problem might easily need a storage of three million entries, and if each entry was equally likely to be the next required the average journey up the tape would be through a million entries, and this would be intolerable. One needs some form of memory with which any required entry can be reached at short notice. This difficulty presumably used to worry the Egyptians when their books were written on papyrus scrolls. It must have been slow work looking up references in them, and the present arrangement of written matter in books is much to be preferred. We may say that storage on tape and papyrus scrolls is somewhat *inaccessible*. It takes a considerable time to find a given entry. Memory in book form is a good deal better, and is certainly highly suitable when it is to be read by the human eye.[11]

The silicon chip, with its solidified information and vast speed of access, answers many of Turing's speculative difficulties about computerised data. But his principal point remains: the book is an extraordinarily handy device.

Foretelling the future is very risky. Go back, for example, and check out Alvin Toffler's *Future Shock* (1970) against 2006. The (then) great futurologist predicted that by now we would be living on oceanic rafts, eating fishburgers and turning the climate on and off like living-room electricity. Among Toffler's other dud predictions is the death of the hardback book, under the pressure of 'information overload'. The book would, he foresaw, melt into the condition of the magazine before dissolving entirely into a ceaseless, impermanent, immaterial 'information flow' – something akin to non-stop muzak in an elevator. But one thing, absent some apocalypse, seems certain. There will be more books – even hardback books – every year. More of the new ones, and more of the old ones which obstinately decline to go away, despite being out of print. With that inexorable increase, new reading and sorting techniques will surely be required.

Judges of fiction prizes are routinely asked if they 'read them all', and are as routinely misreported on the topic. It is hard to reply, accurately, because 'read' is such a blunt term. Is studying *Emma* for A-level the same reading act as skimming the latest Jeffrey Archer in the airport departure lounge with the aim of finishing the thing before boarding in forty minutes? 'I've read the newspaper', we say, meaning ,'I've glanced at the headlines, scanned the letters page, decided not to bother with the editorials, looked up the soccer results and taken in my favourite columnist'. You can gut novels the same way – but it is hardly 'reading'.

Upping the reading speed helps. Silent reading is, although no one is quite sure, a relatively late arrival historically. The Venerable Bede was regarded as prodigious in the seventh century in that he could read without moving his lips and was therefore reading faster than he could speak. What Bede had worked out, evidently, was the amazing buffering capacity of the brain: that it can take in verbiage fast and play it back to the mind's ear at the right, slowed-down speed. Larger 'eyebites' and various other 'speed reading' gimmicks were promulgated in the speed reading mania of the 1960s – when information overload first became a worry. Unfortunately, there are absolute physical limits to the rate at which one can read. Few will reach them, but no human eye will exceed them, any more than any athlete – however well trained and drugged – will run 100 metres in three seconds.

Nowadays, it seems to me, something like the 'surf and zap' approach is required. As with satellite TV and its hundreds of channels, one has to skim through, stop where it seems interesting, zap the commercials and other impertinent material, concentrate from time to time where the offering seems genuinely interesting.

More of this later.

chapter 4

Fiction – a four-minute history

TO BE ABLE to use a novel properly, you should know where the form is coming from historically. It is easier, as it happens, to track than other kinds of book. The novel is the one major literary form whose origins we can confidently, if not quite irrefutably, locate in time and place. Hence its not very original name, the 'new thing'. Poetry and drama are very old things.

In his convincingly argued 1957 critical monograph *The Rise of the Novel*, Ian Watt correlated the historical arrival of fiction as we know it with two other great socio-cultural happenings in Britain: the rise of mercantilist capitalism and, alongside it the ideology of economic and psychological 'individualism'. The foundation text for Watt's thesis was Daniel Defoe's *Robinson Crusoe* (1719).

Robinson, marooned on his island with only his parrot to talk to, but all the wealth of a merchant ship at his disposal, is *homo economicus*. He is Adam Smith's *Wealth of Nations* incarnate – defined entirely by his properties, one of which, of course, is the island and its fruits; another, soon to come into his possession, is his chattel, Man Friday (who, despite the matiness that develops between the two men, will ultimately be sold – business is business). Defoe's novel revolves around inventory of his possessions and wealth, as in the following passage. Robinson has discovered the abandoned wreck of the ship and is removing from it as much booty as he can, by raft, before the vessel sinks:

> I got on board the ship, as before, and prepared a second raft, and having had experience of the first, I neither made this so unwieldy, or loaded it so hard, but yet I brought away several things very useful to me: as first, in the carpenter's stores I found two or three bags full of nails and spikes, a great screw-jack, a dozen or two of hatchets, and above all, that most useful thing called a grindstone; all these I secur'd together, with several things belonging to the gunner, particularly two or three iron crows, and two barrels of musket bullets, seven muskets, and another fowling piece, with some small quantity of powder more; a large bag full of small shot, and a great roll of sheet lead. But this last was so heavy I could not hoist it up to get it over the ship's side.

It is good to know our hero has an ample supply of choppers. But why is all this hardware worth inventorying so pedantically? Because Robinson *is* what he owns. In the capitalist world, property maketh man. Lest we miss its significance, Defoe winds up Robinson's salvage operation, with delicious irony, a page or two on. *Homo economicus* breaks into the captain's safe and finds

> about thirty-six pounds' value in money, some European

coin, some Brasil, some pieces of eight, some gold, some silver. I smiled to myself at the sight of this money. 'Oh drug!' said I aloud, 'What are thou good for? Thou art not worth to me, no, not the taking off the ground; one of those knives is worth all this heap; I have no manner of use for thee, e'en remain where thou art, and go to the bottom as a creature whose life is not worth saving.' However, upon second thoughts, I took it away.

Those second thoughts tell you all you need to know about religion and the rise of capitalism, as the noted social critic R. H. Tawney, anticipating Watt, called it. Robinson will have a bank account on his island – the bank itself (Crusoe plc) will be his as well.

Watt's 'rise of the novel' thesis has been modified and controverted since he wrote it, not least by feminists who point out the male bias in his examples – Defoe, Fielding, Richardson, Sterne, Smollett, etc. There are, women literary historians protest, 'mothers of the novel' as well as fathers (Aphra Behn, for example). There are those, too, with a longer take on things who object that narrative goes as far back as Homer, *Beowulf* and the *Bhagavad Gita*. The novel is merely one side-current in the great tide of human storytelling. In general, however, Watt's thesis seems relatively sound, with whatever small modifications one wishes to make to it.

The coincidence of the rise of the novel with capitalism relates to another of its features. It is a literary form which requires, by way of precondition, a modern industrial and social infrastructure whose elements are mass literacy, disposable wealth among the reading classes, plentiful domestic leisure (one reason that genteel women have always figured in the genre) and the formidable manufacturing capacity which only emerged in Europe in the eighteenth century. You can have poetry, cockfights and the most intricate dance and dramatic performances in a Balinese village. But you cannot have novels.

Novels are expensive to buy. Their new, hardcover, price has consistently been between 5 and 10 per cent of the UK national average weekly wage over the last two centuries. They are also expensive to produce and distribute. They require rapid production of epic quantities of printed matter per title. They require a book world which can review, alert, display and advertise to the consumer, and dispose of and renew its stock many times a year. They require diverse network delivery systems to the end users (libraries, bookshops, book clubs). Those end users have to be both habituated and habitual consumers – good for innumerable repeat orders. The consumer of fiction needs to be educated and literate. The advent of the novel, it is fair to say, required a more sophisticated creation, production, distribution, reception and consumption apparatus than any other cultural form until the arrival, in the 1890s, of the cinema.

The sneer attributed (wrongly, I understand) to the great contemporary American novelist Saul Bellow, 'Where is the Zulu Tolstoy?' could be countered by 'In the same place as the fifteenth-century Saul Bellow'. The novel is the product of a developed, institutionalised and commercially advanced social culture. The ability to read a novel intelligently, I would maintain, is the mark of a mature personal culture. Both have happened very late in world history.

The machinery of book production became industrialised in the nineteenth century. That century was also, as Marx observed in his *Communist Manifesto* (1848), the highpoint of bourgeois hegemony. The novel slipped easily into its linked role as the 'bourgeois epic'. The nineteenth-century novel is to the hegemonic middle classes what the romance was to feudal aristocrats and the ballad to the peasantry. Because of its class ownership, the core of fiction is inherently anti-romantic. Quixotes are found everywhere in its pages, from Henry Fielding's Parson Adams to Salman Rushdie's Saleem Sinai.

In the nineteenth century there emerged what has been called the 'saturation' sales method. Novels are the least predictable of book products in terms of sales. You can very seldom foresee how any single novel will go down with the public – except that some novels (but which?) will fly off the shelves while others will go down the pan as 'returns or remainders' – those most ominous of words to an author's ear. The rule of thumb is, of five novels, three will make a loss for their publisher, one will break even and one will make a profit.

There are a number of ways of shortening the odds. A publisher can pay through the nose for a brand name author who is guaranteed, in so far as such things ever can be, to sell a ton. Or, in the case of a writer like John Grisham, guaranteed to get handsome payments for film or other subsidiary rights, which bounce back as added sales for the book. Hence why Stephen King gets his $30-million multi-book deals. He is that rarest of literary birds: bankable.

Even with the bankable novelists, the margins of profit to the publisher will be whittled down by predatory agents (the nickname of Martin Amis's agent, Andrew 'The Jackal' Wylie, became a household word when he secured a record-breaking advance for his author).[12] You can lose money, even on a sure fire bestseller. Alternatively, rather than stake all your cash on one blockbuster, you can mass-produce fiction for which there is a known, loyal and insatiable fan base. This is how Mills and Boon and Harlequin do it. But even here you can never quite predict the market. And, where the literary rule is me-too-ism, the novels as alike as peas in a pod, and as easy to turn out as widgets, rivals will eat into your market. You cannot trademark and protect a fictional genre.

Another option is to put vast amounts of money into advertising a book – which publishers have long realised to be chancy. A big budget and a lively campaign can boost your novel into the bestseller lists. Perhaps. You can pay booksellers to place your novel in the window, or front of shop, to lure the impulse buyer. You can put pinpoint advertisements in places where the book is most likely to find congenial readers. In the 1990s, for example, publishers realised: a) that people read novels on the London Underground, often keeping a novel going for several days for just that purpose; b) they also read the *Evening Standard* on the Underground. Therefore, put up posters in the Underground stations heavily promoting new novels by the *Standard*'s star columnists, Tony Parsons and Allison Pearson. It worked. The tip was picked up by other publishers with titles likely to appeal to the reader on the tube (it is noticeable that 'literary' stations, such as St John's Wood, tend to have more advertisements for fiction on the walls than, say, West Ham).

The enterprising publisher can use a publicist – a growth branch of the contemporary book trade – to get the author on to talk shows, whip up word-of-mouth and gossip column buzz. But whatever publishers do, however canny and well-funded their campaign, producing novels is always a gamble. Hence why they saturate the market, like the punter who buys a handful of lottery tickets, in the hope that one of the bunch must come up good. One for a certainty *will* – but which?

The late nineteenth century saw the development of the stratifications which still operate in our literary culture: high, middle and low brow; quality fiction and pulp. Genre, or 'category', fiction also emerged (crime, science fiction, romance, porn, westerns, horror, etc.). At its simplest, 'genre' is merely a useful term for where certain known and recognisable varieties of fiction are conventionally shelved in bookshops. At its most complex, genre fiction stakes out new exploratory territories, frequently attracting the most creative minds and most educated (genre-educated, that is) readers. There is still, however, a taint of cultural inferiority. No straight science fiction novel, for example, has ever won a National Booksellers Association award, a Man Booker prize or a Nobel. Was Raymond Chandler a more prizeworthy novelist than John Steinbeck? In my view, yes. Did he win the Nobel? Of course not. More of this later.[13]

Typically, genre fiction is not awarded the dignity of reviews in opinion-forming journals. But it serves as the energy core of fiction, holding together masses of readers, paying, by cross-subsidy, for the quality product. And frequently the lines are blurred – as between Graham Greene's 'novels' (ambitious literary efforts such as *The End of the Affair* (1951)) and what he called 'entertainments' – outright genre works, such as *A Gun for Sale* (1936). This genre quality ambidexterity is continued by writers like Julian Barnes, with his Dan Kavanagh private investigator fictions, or, even more flamboyantly, by Martin Amis (see, for example, his *noir* pastiche, *Night Train* (1997)).[14]

The four minutes is up. The conclusion? Say 'novel' in 1750 and you were, probably, referring to one, or at most a small handful of things. Say 'novel' in 2006, and you could be referring to scores of things.

chapter 5

Targeting – first find your book

The dust jacket is not just for dust

As much as a quarter of the production cost of a hardback novel, publishers tell us, can go on the jacket – an element of the novel which rarely survives as long as the book itself. Typically, the jacket will be the result of the combined efforts of an artist or photographer, contracted from outside, the designer, shrewd in-house publicists and – frequently – the novelist himself, who may well have a hand in the blurb. (With the most prestigious novelists it may be written into the contract that the author has artistic say in the cover design; most are at least consulted.)

Jackets are, in many cases, the first visual encounter its potential buyer will have with a book. First impressions are all-important. Book salesmen typically carry, as their samples, not books but dustjackets and covers. However, while book buyers will make use of such orienting signals as the colour-coding of Penguins, and the livery of 'classic' reprint lines, they tend, in my experience, not to notice much how they, the book buyers, are being influenced by external packaging. It is instructive (and fun) to read this book packaging critically – sceptically, even; to resist, that is, the initial assault on the sensibility.

Take the following case, a strong seller in the early years of the millennium, the paperback edition of Michel Houelle-becq's novel *Atomised*, originally published in French in 1998.

... and, one might add, very sexy

Houellebecq is to the noughties (an appropriate homophone) what Pauline Réage was to the 1960s with *The Story of O*, what Françoise Sagan was to the 1950s with *Bonjour Tristesse*, and what Jean-Paul Sartre was to the 1940s with his *Roads to Freedom* trilogy. The epitome, that is, of Gallic intellectual chic – something that dull Anglo-Americans can only wonder at as they chew the cud of their Georgette Heyer, Herman Wouk or Dick Francis.

Atomised is a novel of ideas and a philosophical analysis of world civilisation in the new millennium. Not for this author the small game. The analysis is bleak. Humanity is in the throes of what Houellebecq labels 'the third mutation'. As the novel's preface puts it:

> Metaphysical mutations – that is to say radical, global transformations in the values to which the majority subscribe – are rare in the history of humanity. The rise of Christianity might be cited as an example. Once a metaphysical mutation has arisen, it tends to move inexorably towards its logical conclusion. Heedlessly, it sweeps away economic and political systems, ethical considerations and social structures. No human agency can halt its progress – nothing but another metaphysical mutation.

There are two truths in the British book trade: translations do badly and books by French intellectuals discoursing on metaphysical mutations, whatever they might be, are not going to set the Thames alight. How, then, should the shrewd British publisher market this intellectually heavyweight but off-putting book? How to grip the purchaser's eyeballs? Answer: the same way that Rupert Murdoch sells the *Sun* – go for the other balls.

That bulge round the pubic region is not, needless to say,

an accurate reflection of the contents of *Atomised*. Some civic-minded person should perhaps invoke the Trades Description Act against the naughty publisher, Vintage. But using women's bodies as cheese on the literary mousetrap has a venerable tradition. Look, for example, at Ace Books' 1950s cover of D. H. Lawrence's *Women in Love* (1921):

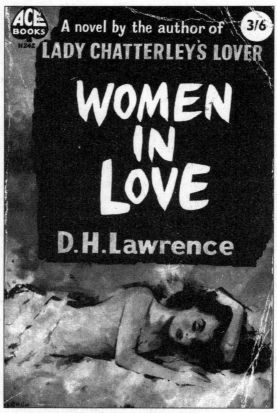

According to the publisher, this volume was very popular with prisoners in the 1950s

The conclusion? If, when you're buying a book, you feel a tender hand on your genitals, the other hand is probably feeling your wallet.

Dust jackets cannot merely advertise a work, or eye-catch. They can — particularly with hardbacks — interpret them. In the example below, Kingsley Amis's sardonic anti-Portnoy polemic *Jake's Thing*, the hero is middle class, late middle-aged with a bad case of erectile dysfunction (a term which would have enraged the jargon-hating novelist, had he lived to hear it).

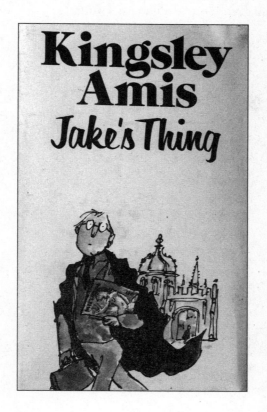

The publisher, Hutchinson, chose to partner Amis with the distinguished illustrator Quentin Blake (famous to generations of children as the creator of the BFG). Blake perfectly catches the twitchy nervousness of the donnish hero, rushing from his Oxford College (clearly identifiable), a skin mag under his gowned arm. Rushing where? The keynote, as Dickens would have said, is struck.

These partnerships between congenial writers and illustrators can extend over several novels, or even the best part of a career, as with Graham Greene and Paul Hogarth, in Penguin's reprints of the novelist's work.

chapter 6

Preliminaries I

COMFORTING AS WILLIAM CAXTON would have found the individual items in the high street bookstore, he would have been overwhelmed by their profusion. In his day, demand exceeded supply – there was an eager, not a sated, market for reading matter, prohibitively expensive as the article was. Even Caxton's lifetime output of some 18,000 printed pages, regarded as formidable in the late fifteenth century, represents less than one day's production in 2006. Well into the 1600s the total number of books, new and old, available to the literate Englishman is reckoned to have been around 2000. If you could afford them (few could), were literate in old and new languages (few were) and lived a long life (few did), you could take in the lot. And a good life it would have been.

Nowadays, books hit the market at the rate of over 2000 titles a week. Unlike baked beans, loaves of bread or Fuji apples, books, once consumed, do not disappear. Despite political legend, they are extremely hard to burn. Books more properly deserve the label 'consumer durables' than refrigerators or cars. Most books look better after seventy years than their owners. Certainly after a hundred they do. 'Consumer imperishables' might be the more accurate term. It is, for some reason, harder, psychologically, to throw away a paperback than a magazine which may have cost as much. They stick around, like literary plaque, clogging up bookshelves and coffee tables. The internet and eBay have boosted the market for pre-owned, pre-read (that is, second-hand) books. A vast number stay in print on the easily accessible backlist ('We don't have it in stock, but we can order it for you, madam' – since the arrival of EPOS, electronic ordering, the request can be filled in hours). There are about three million novels in the British Library, which is being enlarged by some 50,000 new and reissued titles every year. The staff there will deliver any one of them to your desk in St Pancras in hours. And, since the Library's populist reforms of 2005, restrictions on the acquisition of a reader's ticket have been lifted. For any citizen over the age of eighteen the country's major copyright library is liberty hall.

For the reader of novels, it is: Where to start? Is there any point in starting, or shaping one's reading experiences? How can one organise a curriculum? Ours is not, like the 1940s, an age of austerity – state-managed shortage and rationing. It is not money – expensive as new hardback novels, quite irrationally, seem – but time which is in short supply. How, then, to find the novels that you do have the time to invest in? As the science-fiction writer Theodore Sturgeon (the original for Kurt Vonnegut's Kilgore Trout) observed: 'Ninety per cent of science fiction is crap. But 90 per cent of everything is crap.' How can we identify the 10 per cent, or less, of fiction available that is not crap? And while we are on the subject, is Ted Sturgeon's own work crap or caviare?

Confronting the problem in 1909, Arnold Bennett, a great novelist in his day, now almost forgotten, ruled that 'there is only one restriction for you. You must begin with an acknowledged classic; you must eschew modern works.' Bennett was writing a guide to literature called *Literary Taste and How to Form It* for the self-improving British masses, liberated into literacy by the 1870 Universal Education Act. Despite the schoolmasterly tone – one can almost hear the swish of the cane as he lays down the law – the issue remains important. There are, for example, some 500 'best ever' novels available in the Penguin Classics, Oxford World's Classics and Modern Library catalogues. If you prefer the cheap and cheerful Wordsworths, or Signets, without introductions or notes, you can pick up 'acknowledged classics' at a quid a go, or three bucks a pop.

Should a foundation be laid before you go on? It will take years. Or is 'old novel' as much a contradiction in terms as 'new antique'? Surf the present, or shovel up the past? Which is the way to go?

Distasteful as the commodity itself may be, pornography provides a useful model. Smut hounds profile their desired wares according to precise personal preference (S&M, bondage, hard core, gay and lesbian, fetish, etc.) and home in on it like truffle pigs. Readers of fiction should, in their more innocent fashion, do the same. Bookshops used to help. Genre, or 'category fiction', offered bearings for the consumer. Watching browsers (always fascinating) one sees older women drifting towards 'romance', men towards 'male action', older readers towards 'classics', the young towards 'teen fiction'. Bookshops are, in this way, self-mapping. More of this later.

Know your taste

De gustibus, the Latin proverb asserts, non est disputandum. There is no arguing about taste. It is personal. Each of us arrives at, or 'cultivates', our own taste in fiction – and a good thing, too. It may coincide with the taste of others (think of all those Potterheads in Oxford Street on 16 July) but it is none the less ours. In the literary period I know best, the nineteenth century, I have always believed that readers divide into two great taste sectors: Thackerayans, who like fiction which talks, conversationally, to them; and Dickensians, who like their fiction to be theatrical: a spectacle at which they are spectators. One can, of course, appreciate both Vanity Fair and Dombey and Son, as demonstrably many cultivated Victorians did in 1848, when both novels first appeared in monthly serial form, in their rival canary yellow and duck-egg green wrappers. But my guess is that most readers will, in their novel-reading hearts, have had a fond preference for one author's method over the other's.

There is another sense in which we use the term 'taste' – as in wine-tasting, where it has an overtone of 'test', or sample. Bookstores have this wonderful privilege that you can sample (browse), like a cow munching this clump of grass or that, before purchasing. Intelligent browsing remains an essential first step in putting together one's menu. This is not as easy in the United Kingdom as it used to be. Since the abolition in 1995 of the UK Net Book Agreement (that is, retail price maintenance) books have been increasingly shelved, dumped and displayed to catch the purchaser's eye by virtue of reduced (often savagely reduced) price. Publishers now pay, expensively, for front-of-shop placement. This has led, in the highest pressure outlets, to a pervasive decategorisation. It is harder, with all that shouting about bargain price ('Buy now before the men in white coats come and put the manager in a straitjacket'), to find the kind of book that suits you. You are rushed into impulse buying and rushed as precipitately out of the store.

The privilege of browsing is, however, still allowed, if less comfortably than it used to be. The term derives, as has been said, from the eating habits of cattle: ruminant beasts that spend 90 per cent of their waking time peacefully munching and as peacefully digesting: a biteful here, a biteful there; a cowpat here, a cowpat there. This relates to the unique feature of the bookshop: you can sample before you buy (or not). A large proportion of walk-in customers do not know what they want precisely, and will have bought nothing when they leave. They will, none the less, have fingered and sampled the produce, and taken their time doing it. A biteful here, a biteful there. Try, by contrast, going into Tesco's or a Walmart Food Hall and taking chunks out of the Cox's Orange Pippins, the Golden Delicious and the Fuji to determine which kilo of apples you are going to buy today. Or whipping out a tin opener from your pocket and digging into the baked beans, only to decide that you do not, after all, fancy Heinz tonight. Try spending a couple of hours on the service station forecourt, with the nozzle in the tank and then deciding that, well, after all you won't buy any gas today. Maybe tomorrow.

Despite a growing pressure to make bookshops more like In'n' Out Burger, it is still possible to browse. Dustjackets, blurbs, shoutlines, critics' commendations ('quote whores', as they are called in the video/DVD business) all jostle for the browser's attention. But myself, I recommend ignoring the hucksters' shouts and applying instead the McLuhan test. Marshall McLuhan, the guru of *The Gutenberg Galaxy* (1962), recommends that the browser turn to page 69 of any book and read it. If you like that page, buy the book. It works. Rule One, then: browse powerfully and read page 69.

If maps are useful, so are charts. Bestseller lists (available in the US since 1891, and in the UK since 1975) weed down the mass of available novels to the twenty or so that everybody is reading – but almost certainly will not be reading in a few months' time. The trick is not to get into the game late, but to pick the rising titles near the bottom, or to check out what is on the list of the other major English-speaking country before they arrive on your shores.

The downside, of course, is that to follow the charts is to join the thundering herd. I would love, like Dr Johnson, to concur with the common reader; but, at the same time, I want to feel my own person. Uncommon. Getting on for six million copies of *The Da Vinci Code* had sold in the US by April 2006, in the run up to the film, largely because five million copies had already been sold. Better to have been a reader who picked it up when it first appeared at the bottom end of *The New York Times* bestseller list, three years before.

Books published in the Everyman Library, founded by J. M. Dent in 1904, used to carry the Bunyanesque motto: 'Everyman I will go with thee, and be thy Guide' – the implication being, 'Buy the brand [our brand, not Oxford University Press's World's Classics] and get well read'. None the less, every reader yearns for guides. Least reliable, alas, are the reviewers. Not because they are poor judges of quality but because – like the rest of us – they are swamped. Every film that goes on general release in the UK/US will get a whole bunch of reviews. So, too, will every West End or Broadway play. Only some 5 per cent of novels (and virtually no reprinted novels) will be 'noticed'. Big names, of course, will get their front page attention (partly because their publishers can be expected to have taken out advertisements, as they will also have paid booksellers for front-of-store display; if the title is really big, they will additionally have hired an outside publicist to put wheels under the book). The most comprehensive reviews are to be found, inaccessible to the common reader, in the book trade papers: *Publisher's Weekly, Kirkus Review* and *Choice*.

For the unprofessional searcher for the best novel to read, word-of-mouth, intuition, powerful browsing and McLuhan's page 69 test remain the soundest first moves. At the very least, you will make your own mistakes.

Postscript: can you browse electronically?

Do Androids Dream of Electronic Sheep? asked Philip K. Dick, as the title of his witty 1968 sf fable. The leviathan webstores Amazon and Barnes and Noble have functions which they call 'browse'. They also, more illuminatingly, inform you of the books which those who bought the title you are looking at 'also bought'.

The word 'browse' is, of course, metaphorical when applied to what the prospective purchaser does in a bookshop. In an electronic context it is the metaphor of a metaphor. The service which the webstores provide under the term is useful, but it is not, in the received bibliophile sense, browsing.

chapter 7

Closing in

BLURBS — SYNOPSES for the browser/potential buyer began to appear on the dustjackets of books in the early twentieth century. The term is credited to the cartoonist and poet Gelett Burgess, one of whose creations was the overflowing Miss Belinda Blurb. They are typically found on the front flap of a hardback and the back cover of a paperback. One of the things that recommends them as a first port of call for the browser is that they are often written by the authors of the novel themselves. The following blurb for the Picador edition of *The Line of Beauty*, winner of the 2004 Man Booker prize, is, I have been told, from the pen of Alan Hollinghurst himself:

It is the summer of 1983, and young Nick Guest has moved into an attic room in the Notting Hill home of the Feddens: Gerald, an ambitious new Tory MP, his wealthy wife Rachel, and their children Toby and Catherine. Nick had idolized Toby at Oxford, but in his London life it will be the troubled Catherine, the critic and rebel of the family, who becomes both his friend and his uneasy responsibility. As the boom years of the mid-80s unfold, Nick, an innocent in matters of politics and money, becomes caught up in the Feddens' world – its grand parties, its surprising alliances, its parade of monsters both comic and menacing. In an era of endless possibility, Nick finds himself able to pursue his own private obsession, with beauty – a prize as compelling to him as power and riches are to his friends. An affair with a young black council worker gives him his first experience of romance; but it is a later affair, with a beautiful millionaire, that will change his life more drastically and bring into question the larger fantasies of a ruthless decade.

The balance between what is given away of the plot, and what held back, is finely done. And the confident inwardness with what the novel *means* argues either the author's hand, or that of an abnormally sensitive editor.

Easier to come by than the blurb, which has to be sought out, are the aptly named 'shoutlines' and endorsement tags. In the case of paperbacks the latter will usually have been filleted out of reviews. With new hardback novels, they will be either commendations of the author's previous work or solicited pre-publication praise. Whichever, they are useless. Their aim is not to inform but to entice the prospective reader into parting with his money.

Ben Macintyre, writing in *The Times* book supplement on 12 November 2005, recounts an amusing illustration of the worthlessness of endorsement:

Some months ago in this column I made a mildly disobliging remark about a forthcoming novel by Lance

Price, Tony Blair's former spin doctor. Politicians and their acolytes seldom make good novelists, and I was not confident that Mr Price's effort would be any better. I wrote, 'Perhaps *Time and Fate* will be the corking political novel that Blair's Britain so badly needs, but somehow I am doubtful.'

Mr Price's book came out this month, and on the cover appears this ringing endorsement: 'The corking political novel that Blair's Britain so badly needs' – *The Times*.

Macintyre's initial fury subsided into stoical admiration for 'the sheer chutzpah of Mr Price and his publishers'. Chutzpah, yes: that can be found. Reliable guidance as to the book within, probably not.

Even in the most pored-over novels, one page is, typically, never ever read – the copyright page, routinely found on the back of the main title page. It will be crammed with small-print information of primary value to the librarian or bibliographer. Such things as the CIP or ISBN number will probably have no interest for the general reader. Do you know what those acronyms stands for? Do you care?

One piece of information is, however, worth taking note of: the date of the book's first publication and, if it is a reprint, the date of the current printing. This information can be valuable, and occasionally invaluable. Take, for example, the date given in the current Penguin paperback edition of D. H. Lawrence's *Lady Chatterley's Lover*:

First published 1928.
Cambridge University Press edition first published 1993.
Published with new editorial matter in Penguin Books 1994.

PENGUIN BOOKS

Published by the Penguin Group
Penguin Books Ltd, 27 Wrights Lane, London W8 5TZ, England
Penguin Putnam Inc., 375 Hudson Street, New York, New York 10014, USA
Penguin Books Australia Ltd, Ringwood, Victoria, Australia
Penguin Books Canada Ltd, 10 Alcorn Avenue, Toronto, Ontario, Canada M4V 3B2
Penguin Books (NZ) Ltd, Private Bag 102902, NSMC, Auckland, New Zealand

Penguin Books Ltd, Registered Offices: Harmondsworth, Middlesex, England

First published 1928
Cambridge University Press edition first published 1993
Published with new editorial matter in Penguin Books 1994
9 10 8

Copyright © the Estate of Frieda Lawrence Ravagli, 1993
Introduction and Notes copyright © Michael Squires, 1994
Chronology copyright © John Worthen, 1994
All rights reserved

The moral right of the editor has been asserted

Filmset by Datix International Limited, Bungay, Suffolk
Printed in England by Clays Ltd, St Ives plc

Note the literary archaeology

Lawrence's novel is, in terms of its effect on the larger field of fiction, one of the most momentous of the twentieth century – it changed things (although not quite in the way the author wanted). The novel was written and twice rewritten at the end of his life, when Lawrence was an angry man who knew he was dying of consumption and was consumed with hatred for the world he was being forced to exit prematurely. He intended with the novel to blast Anglo-Saxon hypocrisy, and leave a little money for his family.

Lady Chatterley's Lover is as much a testament as a novel. It is also what the Victorians called 'a novel with a purpose' – fiction designed to change the world. More specifically, Lawrence's aim was to hygienise 'four-letter words' and restore them to their Anglo-Saxon purity. And, with this new vocabulary of love ('fucking') the act itself would be purified. One of Lawrence's polemical essays is entitled 'Surgery for the Novel: A Bomb'. This would be his WMD, lobbed into the cosy world of British fiction. Post-*Lady Chatterley's Lover*, British fiction would never be the same again.

Brutally summarised, the novel is the story of an aristocrat, Sir Clifford Chatterley, who has been rendered paraplegic, and sexually neutered, in the Great War (the war which, Lawrence believed, had destroyed European culture for ever, as a tree is destroyed when its roots are torn up). Sir Clifford returns, crippled, confused and castrated, to his estate in the Midlands, where he has coal mines and a stately home. But the aristocracy, which he represents, no longer has authority. Clifford's wife, Connie, falls in love with her husband's gamekeeper. (The plot inspired one of the crispest dismissals in literary history, from *The Field and Stream Magazine*: 'In this reviewer's opinion this book cannot take the place of J. R. Miller's *Practical Gamekeeping*.')

Connie and Mellors embark on a rampantly physical adulterous affair, in which Lawrence's newly hygienised lexicon of love is given uninhibited expression (Mellors, it should be explained, lapses from received pronunciation into his native Derbyshire when naked with Connie. She retains the accents of a titled lady – even when, as happens late in the narrative, her lover anally rapes her):

'Let me be. I like thee. I luv when tha lies theer. A woman's

a lovely thing whe 'er's deep ter fuck, and cunt's good. Ah
luv thee, thy legs, an' th' shape on thee, an' th' womanness
on thee. Ah luv thee wi' my ba's and wi' my heart.'

This kind of prose, however high-minded its purpose,
was unpublishable in Britain and America in 1928. It was the
period when Anthony Comstock's Society for the Suppression
of Vice had an iron hand on literature in the United States.
In Britain, the puritanical Home Secretary Joynson Hicks
– 'The Lord's Policeman' – presided over a similarly censo-
rious regime which in the same year that Lawrence finished
Lady Chatterley's Lover banned as obscene 'John' (birth name
Marguerite) Radclyffe Hall's *The Well of Loneliness*, a novel
with no four-letter words, but with nights of steamy passion
between lesbians euphemistically described.

Suppressing fiction seems another example of the law
and the ass. But, historically, books, even novels, have
demonstrated a powerful capacity to unsettle, and even help
overthrow, the state. The state is not necessarily asinine in
being wary of them. In *The Forbidden Best-sellers of Pre-Revo-
lutionary France*, Robert Darnton traces how underground
pornography (in which category many at the time would have
placed Voltaire's novel *Candide*), by scurrilously ridiculing
the Church and the nobility, corroded the moral fabric of the
ancien régime. Lawrence's novel, about a servant diddling the
wife of a member of the aristocracy, raised the same fears in
the interwar British establishment. Their turn in the tumbril
had come.

Lady Chatterley's Lover came out in an authorised edition in
Italy in 1928 and various pirated editions in Paris soon thereafter. Without the benefit of international copyright, it could
not be protected. His tale of jolly rogering had been jolly

rogered, Lawrence declared, by way of a deathbed quip. An expurgated version was published posthumously in America, to establish copyright – but brought no income to the estate. Another brutally expurgated version came out in the late 1940s in Britain and the United States. Lawrence, as he said, would no more have sanctioned such expurgated texts ('it bleeds') than he would have allowed his fingers to be cut off in the interest of satisfying Mrs Grundy.

For the best part of thirty years, *Lady Chatterley's Lover*, less its Anglo-American figleaves, was an offshore bestseller, most conveniently available in France. Reading the novel in Paris and, if you were extremely daring, smuggling it back into Britain, was a rite of passage for schoolboys like myself in the 1950s (there were, it may be recorded, many more aphrodisiac products catering for every 'preference' to be had from the catalogue of M. Girodias, but 'Lady Chat' was the most notorious).

In 1959–60 Grove Press in America and Penguin Books in the UK resolved to bring *Lady Chatterley's Lover* back into respectable, Anglophone literary existence. In a series of high-profile trials, assisted by liberalising legislation and the newly admissible evidence of 'expert witnesses', they succeeded. In America, for a wild few months in 1960, Lawrence's novel remained unprotected by copyright and was ruthlessly plundered. At one particularly low point it was being sold on street corners in Boston, the citadel of American censorship, for 25 cents in newspaper form. Eventually international copyright protection for the book was established.

Lady Chatterley's Lover eventually made a lot of money for its intrepid producers and Lawrence's heirs. More importantly, it redefined permissibility for the practising novelist. If, for example, Kingsley Amis had chanced his arm in 1954 with a passage like this, twenty years on, from his son Martin's *Dead Babies* (1975), *Lucky Jim* would never have seen it into print:

> 'How big's his cock, for instance?' inquired Diana, settling herself on the window-seat and placing the tea-tray on Celia's crowded dressing table.
>
> Celia winced as she strained to unscrew a jar of face-cream. 'Pretty big. Well above average. Ah, thank you, Diana. How big's Andy's?'
>
> Diana sighed. 'Enormous. When he's not on anything of course.' She sipped her tea, and asked, peering over her cup, 'How often does Quentin fuck you?'
>
> With white-plumed fingertips Celia dabbed at her variegated, spot-sprinkled face. The clear fact that Celia's complexion was so much worse than her own slightly mitigated her disgust when Celia said, 'Once a night, at least. And usually in the morning.'

So, too, with Norman Mailer. His first published novel, *The Naked and the Dead*, a powerful chronicle of war in the Pacific, was a ground-breakingly daring book for its time – that time being 1947. Determined to represent, as best the literary *mores* would allow him, how the country's marines actually spoke, Mailer larded his dialogue with the word 'fug' (it inspired the wisecrack from Dorothy Parker, 'So *you're* the young man who can't spell fuck?')

But Mailer could never, in pre-Chatterley 1947, have published what he wrote in post-Chatterley 1965, in *An American Dream*, describing the hero – almost casually – deciding to anally rape his wife's German maid before, just as casually, murdering her:

I wanted more and more, and so I slipped free of her

mouth and put her on her back. But then, as abruptly as an arrest, a thin high constipated smell (a smell which spoke of rocks and grease and the sewer-damp of wet stores in poor European alleys) came needling its way out of her. She was hungry, like a lean rat she was hungry, and it could have spoiled my pleasure except that there was something intoxicating in the sheer narrow pitch of the smell which could be mellowed only by the gift of fur and gems, she was money this girl, she cost money, she would make money, something as corrupt as a banquet ... I had a desire suddenly to skip the sea and mine the earth, a pure prong of desire to bugger, there was canny hard-packed evil in that butt, that I knew. But she resisted, she spoke for the first time, 'Not there! *Verboten!*'

But resistance, as a less raunchy novelist, Douglas Adams, would put it, is futile.

Publication of *Lady Chatterley's Lover*, timed by Penguin to coincide with the thirtieth anniversary of Lawrence's death, marked the novelist's return to high respectability. This respectability was crowned by Cambridge University Press undertaking a total re-editing and reissuing of the major works. In this honorific series, *Lady Chatterley's Lover* was published in 1993. The scholarly editing, and new matter from manuscript remains, constituted a new copyright. All this lies behind that apparently insignificant entry on the novel's copyright page, 'First published 1928. Cambridge University Press edition first published 1993. Published with new editorial matter in Penguin Books 1994.'

The pre-Chatterley, post-Chatterley 1960 break falls, like Joseph Conrad's shadow line, across the careers of authors like Philip Roth (compare *Goodbye, Columbus* (1959), with his outrageous homage to onanism, *Portnoy's Complaint* (1969)),

Mary McCarthy (*The Groves of Academe* (1952) and *The Group* (1963)), or Brian Aldiss (compare the space-operatic *Starship* (1958) with his outrageous homage to onanism, *The Hand-Reared Boy* (1970)).

In summary, a wise rule is: turn over the title page to look at the date and the publication history, and then do a little digging. It is not much encouraged. Reprint publishers are rarely keen to advertise, for example, that Philip Roth's 2006 reissue of *Goodbye, Columbus* is somewhat less fresh on the shelf than the author's hot-off-the-press *The Plot against America* (2005).

The case of dates and *Lady Chatterley's Lover* raises another complicated issue. The narrative opens with a much-quoted Lawrentian diatribe:

> Ours is essentially a tragic age, so we refuse to take it tragically. The cataclysm has happened, we are among the ruins, we start to build up new little habitats, to have new little hopes. It is rather hard work: there is now no smooth road into the future: but we go round, or scramble over the obstacles. We've got to live, no matter how many skies have fallen.

In their headlong rush to get to the 'bouts', many in 1960 may have idly wondered when 'our age' was precisely. It is clearly key to the narrative that follows. 'Our age' is manifestly not 1959–60, when the Penguin edition became available to the mass of English speaking readers. Nor, if one reads on carefully, is the novel set in the late 1920s, when Lawrence wrote it. *Lady Chatterley's Lover* is set, like *The Great Gatsby*, at the dawn of the 'jazz age' – that Dionysian period in the early 1920s before the General Strike in 1926 in Britain and the

1929 stock market collapse in the US ushered in apocalypse and 'worldwide crack-up', as Fitzgerald called it. 'There's black days coming – for us all and for everybody,' says Mellors 'prophetically'. He is foreseeing the late 1920s, the period in which Lawrence actually wrote the novel, and during which he was living (and dying).

If not quite 'historical', the action of *Lady Chatterley's Lover* is 'dated'. Reading the novel in 2006 requires a number of delicate tunings of one's perceptions, both to discriminate and then to take on board a whole series of 'nows'. One has to inject the terminal pessimism of the author's 1928, as he coughed his way to the grave and the decade (with slump and fascism imminent) came to its sorry end; and then go back to a Gatsby-esque early 1920s, which Lawrence saw as something equivalent to Edgar Allan Poe's Masque of the Red Death. A scandalous 'dirty novel' in the 1930s, *Lady Chatterley's Lover* was a high-minded taboo-breaker in the 1960s and – amazingly – a canonical text set on university courses and a BBC 'Book at Bedtime' in the 1990s, while the dramatisation of the trial, with all the four-letter words, became a prime-time television drama in 2006. As for offensiveness, Lawrence's novel is positively tame for sensibilities calloused by *American Psycho*. All this must be understood in order to properly appreciate the significance of the work's complicated passage through literary time, from dirty book to classic.[15]

Framing fiction within the necessary time and culture settings is tricky and requires practice. But without that framework, something will be seriously missing. And, as step one, it pays to go to the first (and subsequent) publication dates inscribed on the copyright page and work on from there. If possible, find out when the novel was a) conceived, b) written and c) set – and then throw them all into the mix.

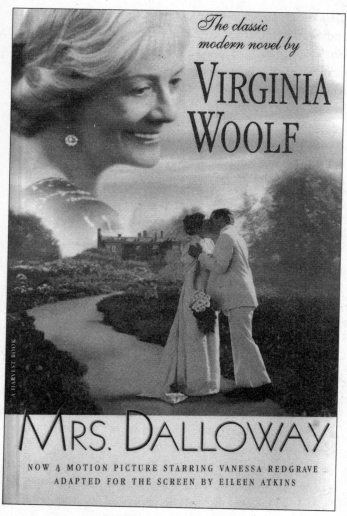

The classic modern novel by

VIRGINIA WOOLF

A HARVEST BOOK

MRS. DALLOWAY

NOW A MOTION PICTURE STARRING VANESSA REDGRAVE
ADAPTED FOR THE SCREEN BY EILEEN ATKINS

Woolf gets the Hollywood treatment

There are many other examples which press home the point. It is difficult to make full sense of Mrs Dalloway if you do not register that, although the novel was published in 1925, it was conceived and written three years earlier, in the utterly exhausted convalescence after the Great War and the great Spanish flu pandemic (the heroine, Clarissa Dalloway, is still slowly recovering from both afflictions). Nor will Woolf's last novel, Between the Acts, make much sense if you do not know that it was written during the early days of the Second World War, which thinking Britons quite expected to lose, and set in a terminal 1939 (the novel's posthumous publication followed hard on the author's suicide in 1941). Registering that mood, of course, requires not merely an act of historical reconstruction but also the effort of working against the residue of images, many misleading, which a great novel accumulates in its long life – longer, inevitably, than that of its creator. The film version of Mrs Dalloway (1997) inspired a tie-in paperback whose romanticised cover is as remote from Spanish Flu and the Great War, as it is from Mars.

Novels have their chronological climates – sometimes more than one, layered each on top of the other. John Grisham's The Firm, the novel which made him a superseller, was published in 1991. But why, in the legal (in fact Mafia front) firm in which the hero, Mitch McDeere, finds himself are there no desktop computers? Why does Mitch, a high-flying legal eagle, not have a cell phone, as even junior school kids had by the early 1990s? Because, I suspect, the novel had been written some years before and was a long time in finding a publisher. The techno-lag was lavishly amended in the 1993 movie of the book starring Tom Cruise. The filmic McDeere is wholly geared up, technologically unlike his print-hobbled alter ego.

There are any number of examples where dates of conception and first publication, and some basic information of what they mean historically, are not merely useful or thought-provoking but essential. *Middlemarch*, for example, is often cited by writers and celebrities as 'the novel that changed my life'. But unless the reader appreciates that *Middlemarch* is set in the period of the first Reform Bill (1832), but was conceived by George Eliot and published by John Blackwood (political conservatives both) in the immediate aftermath of the second Reform Bill (1867), the political urgency of the work – more specifically, its peculiar mix of high Victorian liberal-conservatism – will be missed. It becomes merely 'historical' in the long-ago-and-far-away sense of the term.

One of the shortcomings of Andrew Davies's otherwise excellent 1994 television adaptation of *Middlemarch* was that it did not communicate the fact that George Eliot was writing thirty years on from the 1830-ish events depicted. It could have been done with a prefatory scene (the novelist in her 1870 study, for example, with a portrait of Prime Minister Gladstone on the wall). But that would have detracted from the in-the-viewer's-face immediacy of the narrative – a quality which television, with its tight time units, values more highly than does the printed novel. Particularly a novel as vastly loose-knit and leisurely in its progression as Eliot's.

A great virtue of the recent spate of television/movie adaptations of fiction classics is their identifying – principally by dress, hairstyle and decor – precise historical periods. But even here things can go wrong. The many recent adaptations of *Pride and Prejudice* have invariably tended to draw on the fashions of the Regency period: partly, perhaps, because the fashions are beautiful and pleasing to the contemporary eye; partly because the novel was published in 1813, the

Miss Bennet in full Regency finery

second year of the Regency. But the novel is actually set in the mid 1790s, when Britain was at war with Revolutionary France (hence all those soldiers – invasion was expected). *Pride and Prejudice*, initially provisionally called 'First Impressions', antedates its publication by some seventeen years. To 'Regencify' *Pride and Prejudice* is as anachronistic an error as to have a V2 bomb land on Joe Lampton's Brylcreemed head in *Room at the Top* (1954).

'Regencification' (to repeat the ugly word) in the cause of making Keira Knightley yet more delectable is, the reader may think, a good thing. It can, however, be overdone as in the accompanying 1934 Novel Library one-shilling edition of *Jane Eyre* (snappily re-titled), designed to piggy-back the PDC, low-budget film (starring the less than starry Virginia Bruce and Colin Clive – not, definitely not, to be confused with the 1944 Orson Welles, Joan Fontaine version of Charlotte Brontë's novel).

Jane Eyre *for the people*

One of the oddities of literature is that we can still be wholly gripped, transported even, by novels which history has shown to be entirely wrong. The year 1984, in the event, turned out to be nothing at all like *Nineteen Eighty-Four* (although, as pedants like to point out, Orwell's future is suspiciously like 1948, the year in which he was writing his novel). Take, as another chronological peculiarity, the opening to Arthur C. Clarke's classic science-fiction story *The Sands of Mars*, first published in 1951:

> 'So this is the first time you've been upstairs?' said the pilot, leaning back idly in his seat so it rocked back and fro in the gimbals. He clasped his hands behind his neck in a nonchalant manner that did nothing to reassure his passenger.
>
> 'Yes,' said Martin Gibson, never taking his eyes from the chronometer, as it ticked the seconds.

The two men, pilot and passenger, are a thousand kilometres from earth, *en route* to Mars, in the spaceship *Ares*. It is the early years of the twenty-first century (that is, now). Such trips are as routine as the Eurostar service from London to Paris – and scarcely more expensive for the passenger. Quite clearly, in terms of technological forecast, Clarke's future is comically unlike what we see around us in 2006. What he projects is a BOAC (now British Airways) cockpit, in one of those new-fangled Comet jet airliners, manned by British 'pilots'. American and Russian astronauts never happened. Nor did the sheer difficulty (verging on impossibility) of manned flight to neighbouring planets.

In the immediate post-war period, when Britain was still one of the 'Big Three' (as the United States, the Soviet Union and the United Kingdom were called), Clarke's fantasy was plausible. The Union Jack would be up there in space with the Stars and Stripes and the Hammer and Sickle. Equally plausible, given the huge advance in rocketry pioneered by the Nazis at Peenemunde, was the fantasy of interplanetary travel becoming as routine as a commute between Virginia Water and Waterloo or Long Island and Grand Central. Judged historically (as, in time, all futuristic fiction will come to be judged) Clarke's scenario is plain wrong. Comically so ('ticking chronometer'? – what next, egg-timers?). But this quaint failure to get it right has never affected Clarke's standing as a patriarchal figure in science fiction – one of its 'Big Three' (along with Asimov and Heinlein). *The Sands of Mars* is still in print and is still honoured as one of the genre's canonical texts. More to the point, it can still – despite its wrongness – be enjoyed by twenty-first-century readers who are able to reset their literary 'chronometers' and adjust their literary 'gimbals' to read the work in two time contexts.[16]

chapter 8

Preliminaries II

ONE OF THE more consequential marks applied to all contemporary fiction is the © [that is, copyright] symbol. While not immediately useful to the reader, like the publication date(s), the mark is worth a moment's meditation. It is highly informative. Without that small device and what it legally denotes – that is, copyright ownership – the novel would never have been viable as a literary form. It is no accident that the novel came into being after the Queen Anne copyright act of 1710, the first in the world. In one of the more challenging paradoxes of literary criticism, the Marxist Walter Benjamin declared that the rise of the novel meant the end of storytelling. Storytelling received its death sentence with the invention of copyright. Copyright did to storytelling what the eighteenth century's enclosures did to the English countryside.

Benjamin's argument runs thus. If I tell you a story and you pass it on to a friend by the usual Chinese whispers effect it will be the same story but different. Each teller will, as the story circulates, make large or small changes to the narrative.[17] The joke, particularly the dirty joke (or, as it used to be called, the 'smoking room' joke) is a case in point. An unexpectedly successful film in 2005 was *The Aristocrats*, in which a score of American comedians tell, in their own distinctive way, what is generally regarded as the filthiest joke in the jokester's library. (Essentially it involves a circus family indulging in the vilest and most bizarre sexual practices imaginable. When asked what they intend to call their new act, they blandly reply: 'The Aristocrats'.) What is striking about the film is that every comedian tells the joke differently – markedly differently. Yet it is, recognisably, the 'same' joke. The novel, by contrast, is frozen in its single authorised form. The text of Evelyn Waugh's 1945 homage to the British aristocracy, *Brideshead Revisited*, is immutable. A whole academic editorial industry has grown up dedicated to establishing the single 'authoritative' text of classic works. Copyright law will no more allow you to change them than the carabinieri would let you take a hammer and Polyfilla to Michelangelo's *David* and tart it up a bit.

Ownership is what it all comes down to. Jokes like 'The Aristocrats' have no 'owners'. They float free in the public domain. Typically, no one even knows where such jests originate – if, indeed, they have a single creator. Dirty jokes, it used to be thought, were devised in prisons by inmates with nothing better to do – they rose, in other words, from the sewers of our society. Novels, by contrast, have very clearly defined legal originators and owners: the author, who created the 'work' and owns the copyright; the publisher who has bought and has contractually licensed the sole right to publish the 'work' in a certain territory or format; the retail merchan-diser who owns the physical commodity the publisher has produced (an author, for example, will be prosecuted for shoplifting if he goes into Waterstone's and helps himself to a copy of 'his' book); the customer who owns the commodity the retailer has sold him. All that sequence of ownership is inherent in the little mark ©. And it is what makes a novel different from a story.

The copyright cramp on the novel is, however, compensated for by a great freedom. There is no copyright in ideas, merely in the linguistic form in which those ideas are expressed. Here, an author may reap where he has not sown. This means that plotlines, scenarios, character types, gimmicks are all there for the taking. A new idea in fiction, if it catches on, will quickly be snapped up by other writers. Take, for example, the alternative, or parallel, universe gimmick often used in science fiction. The pioneer is generally taken to be Ward Moore, whose *Bring the Jubilee* (1953) fantasises an America in which the South won the Civil War, existing in some neighbouring universe alongside ours in which, of course, the North won. This was picked up by Philip K. Dick in one of the greatest of science fiction novels, *The Man in the High Castle* (1962), in which in one universe Japan won the war and in another, the Allies – characters slip between the two. Since then there have been any number of creative plunderings of Moore's alternative universe gimmick: Len Deighton's *SS–GB* (1978), in which Germany won the Second World War, and Robert Harris's *Fatherland* (1992) (ditto) are two bestselling examples. In Kingsley Amis's witty *The Alteration* (1976), the Reformation was unsuccessful, and contemporary Britain is still in thrall to Rome and the Catholic Church. In the 1960s–90s, the alternative universe gimmick became a standby of the 'Doctor Who' children's TV series. Were such gimmicks (or what Henry James called '*données*') patentable, like Xerox or Microsoft technology, Ward Moore and his estate would be a lot richer but science fiction a lot poorer.

The 'no copyright in ideas' freedom may be under threat. In 2001, the estate of Margaret Mitchell moved to have a burlesque of *Gone with the Wind* suppressed. Called *The Wind Done Gone*, Alice Randall's spoof retold *Gone with the Wind* from a slave's viewpoint. Randall, herself an African-American, was sardonically reminding readers that Mitchell's novel (unlike the film, which MGM carefully sanitised) has admiring sections on the Klu Klux Klan (with whom Rhett rides) and diatribes against post-bellum 'uppity darkies'. The Mitchell estate's argument was, as I understand it, that *Gone with the Wind* was not a novel but a franchise, like McDonald's or Burger King, and a veritable industry based on intellectual property which could be protected by patent or trademark. *The Wind Done Gone* was duly injuncted, and the injunction lifted after the novel's publishers, Houghton Mifflin, made an out of court settlement with the Mitchell estate. The © may, it seems possible, be replaced by ™ at some future date and novelists' freedom to reap where they have not sown may be curtailed. It would be a serious loss.

chapter 9

Titles

THERE IS, ODDLY, no copyright in titles. Thus in 2005 Ben Elton could publish a novel about war called *The First Casualty*, alluding to the proverb about truth in wartime, with no legal offence to Philip Knightley, whose earlier history of British journalism in wartime has exactly the same smart title. But, inviting as it might be (*The Da Vinci Code* by Jeffrey Archer) such duplication is infrequent – librarians, booksellers, authors and readers themselves dislike it too much. It creates confusion.

Once browsers have homed in on a particular section of the bookshop (or less often nowadays, the library), titles play an important role – particularly if would-be readers are in the familiar situation of not knowing what they want but knowing they want *something*. That something may be elusive – adding, in a sedate way, the thrill of the hunt to the act of browsing (it is heightened to the thrill of the treasure hunt in a second-hand bookshop, where *anything* may turn up). A town centre bookshop can have as many as 100,000 'titles' in stock and five times as many on call – as against, say, six new models and twenty salesmen to help you in the nearby car showroom.

Unlike in supermarkets (however much they are coming to resemble them) in bookshops there is also the self-digni-fying feeling that by your purchase you are, in a sense, making a statement about yourself. It is noticeable, for example, that customers queuing up to buy books are very curious, discreetly peeking all the while, about what the others in the queue are buying, in a spirit of subdued rivalry. At the Tesco or Safeways check-out line, you do not care in the slightest whether the person in front has smart organic baked beans or the supermarket's own cheap brand, so long as their cart is not heaped so mountainously high that you will be waiting all day for the till.

Titles, and title pages, were historically a relatively late development in the apparatus of the codex book. Chaucer, for example, did not call his fourteenth-century text of the Canterbury tales *The Canterbury Tales*. Titles were invented for the same reason as were ISBNs (International Standard Bar Code Numbers) in the 1970s – to give books a recognisably separate identity. They have titles for the same reason that soldiers and dogs have dog-tags, so that they can be iden-tified, by merchandisers, distributors and owners, from the ruck of other books. No ruck, as in Chaucer's day, no titles.

But there is a fundamental difference between the reader's encounter with a novel and with most other kinds of book. With those other kinds you usually know, ahead of time, the content and where – once the reading is embarked on – you are going. The title (*How to Read a Novel*, for example) typically tells us. It is self-referencing, as indexers say. Novels, other than consciously out-of-step novels (such as Philip Hensher's

2004 story of a melancholic indexer, *The Fit*) don't have indexes, nor, necessarily, do they have self-referencing titles. However, they can, of course, have titles which make the contents as clear as day. There is little enigma in the title of Mrs Craik's 1856 fable of Smilesian, clogs-to-mill-owner self-help, *John Halifax Gentleman*. A bestseller for half a century, and a favourite Sunday School giftbook, Craik's novel follows the hero's admirable rise from worthy working-class origins to gentlemanhood. But Craik clearly chose her declaratory title so as to get through to a certain kind of inexpert reader of fiction (children and servants, principally). As with the religious tract ('The sinner's straight way to Hell'), for her there should be no ambiguity as to the moral message. The title is a punchline. Many novel titles are more like ju-jitsu – they lead the prospective purchaser to trip over their feet.

There is helpful apparatus found in other kinds of book missing from the novel. Novels typically lack explanatory tables of contents which the reader, or prospective reader, can scan ahead of time. Again, of course, they can have them. Many readers will have had reason to be profoundly grateful, for example, that Samuel Richardson added a synoptic summary of chapter contents to the third edition of his massive *Clarissa*. For instance:

LETTER I. Miss Howe to Miss Clarissa Harlowe.–
Desires from her the particulars of the rencounter between Mr Lovelace and her brother; and of the usage she receives upon it: also the whole of her story from the time Lovelace was introduced as a suitor to her sister Arabella. Admires her great qualities, and glories in the friendship between them.

There is no reason in nature that prevents other novelists following Richardson's example. But extremely few choose to do so.

Chapter titles have at various periods of fiction been popular. Richardson's great rival, Henry Fielding, was addicted to them – as in *Tom Jones* (VII, 4), 'In which is introduced one of the pleasantest barbers that ever was recorded in History'. The Victorians also liked them – as they did running titles over the page summarising the plot in more detail as they went along. Such devices keep a novel in order – they 'fence' it. Some twentieth-century writers, notably Evelyn Waugh, used chapter titles with great art – often as a kind of ironic miasma, or protracted sneer, which permeated the narrative below. The first chapter of *A Handful of Dust*, that 1934 satire on the terminal decay of English civility, is entitled: 'Du Côté de Chez Beaver' (that is to say, 'This is not Proust, my friend').

In general the chapter title has been little used by novelists in the last hundred years. An exception is Martin Amis, who seems to like them – because, as with Waugh, they offer an opportunity for some local authorial cleverness. *Time's Arrow* (1991), Amis's Holocaust novel, is a reverse deathbed-to-womb narrative, following (backwards) the life of a war criminal who escapes justice by going underground in America with the help of 'Odessa', the clandestine Nazi group which Frederick Forsyth made famous in his 1972 novel with a title reminiscent less of fiction than of an MI5 top-secret report, *The Odessa File*. Amis's first chapter title is the Jewish proverb 'What goes around comes around': in context, this stalest of truisms is multi- and razor-edged. Other chapter titles in *Time's Arrow* (Such as 'Because Ducks are Fat') tend, if anything, to compound the vertiginously unsettling effect. It adds to the unsettlement that the title of the novel refers to a complicated thesis in theoretical physics.

If a book has chapter titles, then they are worth scanning before purchase, or before investing reading time in it. So, too, with prefaces and afterwords (*Time's Arrow* contains one listing Amis's direct influences, which is very useful). But expect to find no clear guidance.

Chances are, however, that titles, wherever found, will not tell you what you really want to know. The novelist's palm must be crossed with silver before it yields its message; and sometimes the book has to be read and thought about before the title becomes at all comprehensible. If then. Go to the computer software section of the bookstore and the manuals on C++, TurboPascal or PhotoShop will leave you in no doubt as to their contents. If you are not sure, the title will go out of its way to be helpful (*Windows XP for Dummies*, for example).

With novels it is different. Hence such hoary bookstore jokes as:

'Excuse me, young man, where will I find *Cancer Ward*?'
'Try the medical section, madam.'
'How can I get *White Teeth*?'
'Brush three times a day, madam.'
'*Black Beauty*?'
'Could be in ethnic studies, sir.'
'Where is Martin Amis's *Money*?'
'In Coutts's bank, I imagine, madam. He's been selling rather well recently – although *Time's Arrow* proved a little off-putting for some of our readers.'

Novels can throw out the most baffling titular signals, rather like in the early days of the Second World War when, to confuse the invading Hun, rural signposts in England were turned the wrong way round. Take, for example, a master of the enigmatic title, Graham Greene. *The Comedians* (1965), the unwary reader will discover, is an extremely un-amusing novel set in the Hell of Papa Doc's Haiti in the 1960s. What, pray, is to laugh at in a passage like the following, describing a naive American philanthropist making a trip to the local post office?:

> Mr Smith had been in the republic a week now. He had seen the kidnapping of Doctor Philpot's body; I had driven him through the worst of the shanty-town. That morning he had insisted against my advice in going to the Post-Office himself to buy stamps. I had lost him momentarily in the crowd, and when I found him again he had not been able to approach a foot towards the *guichet*. Two one-armed men and three one-legged men hemmed him round. Two were trying to sell him dirty old envelopes containing out of date Haitian postage-stamps: the others were more frankly begging. A man without legs at all had installed himself between his knees and removed his shoe-laces preparatory to cleaning his shoes. Others seeing a crowd collected were fighting to join it. A young fellow, with a hole where his nose should have been, lowered his head and tried to ram his way through towards the attraction at the centre. A man with no hands raised his pink polished stumps over the heads of the crowd to exhibit his infirmity to the foreigner. It was a typical scene in the Post-Office except that foreigners were rare nowadays.

Very comical.

Greene's *Brighton Rock* (1938) is an elephant trap for those not familiar with the seaside town's flat and shingly shores. Given the author's international appeal there must be many such. I recall in the 1950s seeing a *livre de poche* translation (*Les Rochers de Brighton*) which portrayed on its cover a mighty cliff face as sheer and lofty as the Eiger. The French – who gave us a whole lexicon of *bon-bon* words – have, I believe, no exact term for the homely suck-it-and-see tubular candy which has 'Brighton' (or 'Margate', or 'Skegness') indelibly inscribed, in scarlet, across its saccharine circumference. Seaside rock is not that easily come by in Britain nowadays, and has always been a source of mystery to American readers, of whom the novelist has many. Why, in a novel which ends with murder and 'final horror' on a clifftop, did Greene call it that, rather than, say, 'Licorice Allsorts' or 'Polo Mint'? Read it and see.

The End of the Affair (1951) could mean the wrapping-up of some trifling business (a quarrel with the tax man, a spat over room charges), or the end of something akin to *Madame Bovary*. In fact, it is both. The story centres on a banal adultery, a mystery as to where a married woman is spending her afternoons and the gobsmackingly blasphemous end of a love affair in which God Almighty is portrayed as the co-respondent – as the courts of the time in which the novel is set would have put it. But, ironically (Greene is ever ironic), at the end of the novel, which is the opening, nothing is actually ended. Nor, as the opening line portentously declares, is anything ever truly 'begun':

> A story has not beginning or end: arbitrarily one chooses that moment of experience from which to look back or from which to look ahead.

In many cases, the title does not make sense until you have read the novel. And even then you may not be 100 per cent sure what the thing means. Which of the lovers, for instance, was 'Pride' and which was 'Prejudice'? Personally I have never quite been able to make up my mind. Darcy is inordinately proud of being Mr Darcy of Pemberton and appallingly prejudiced against countryfied girls with no background, such are to be found at a Meryton 'rout'. Elizabeth, however, is prejudiced against proud stuck-up people who think they are better than the gentry of Longbourn.

In Lawrence's *Sons and Lovers* (1913), why 'sons', since the novel seems to be almost entirely concerned with Paul and Mrs Morel? Why did Virginia Woolf call her 1927 book *To the Lighthouse*, rather than 'The Lighthouse', or, if she had wanted to be crystal clear, 'Sailing to the Lighthouse' (as with Yeats's poem, 'Sailing to Byzantium' (1926))? The preposition is vaguely unsettling – a mote to trouble the mind's eye. Why did Dickens call his 1846–8 novel *Dombey and Son* when, as readers often point out, the novel is more appropriately 'Dombey and Daughter'? Why don't *Howards End* and *Finnegans Wake* have apostrophes? Are the authors, as the critics instruct us, masters of the genre or greengrocer'[sic]s? Why did Anthony Burgess call his 1962 novel *A Clockwork Orange*? The reader will search the text in vain for a clue. The only hint is that the unnamed writer whom Alex and his droogs subject to horrific home invasion is writing a book called *A Clockwork Orange*. But that book, on the sample given, is nothing like the novel the unlucky writer finds himself in. Burgess himself gave some equivocal assistance in an interview. A connoisseur of street talk, he said that he once overheard a cockney say that someone was 'queer as a clockwork orange' (but not, Burgess went on to say, 'queer' in the sense of homosexual). The simile had stuck in his mind. Why he went on to stick it on his novel is unclear.

There is a theory that *The Da Vinci Code*, first published

in 2003, started its slow burn to perennial bestsellerdom because for those reading it in, say, an airport departure lounge Brown's book could masquerade as a respectable tome on Renaissance art. Had the author called it 'Spawn of Jesus', the novel might have joined 95 per cent of the thriller genre in oblivion. Who would want to be seen reading that?

Titles, it seems, often set out to inaugurate a game between author and reader – a game which, if the novel works, will add immensely to the reader's pleasure. If the novel does not work, it will simply be something else to cheese the reader off. Detective novels in particular relish titular game play. Agatha Christie's *Murder on the Orient Express* (1934) supplies the reader from the kick-off with two of the plot's main elements Question: What? Answer: Capital crime. Question: Where? Answer: On a transcontinental train. But Christie's title withholds the third and most critical piece of information. Whodidit?

Although commonest in that genre, the teasingly incomplete title is by no means a monopoly of the crime writer. When Henry James called his novel *What Maisie Knew* he effectively challenged the reader to come up with an answer. That answer is, however, more complicated than Poirot's identifying who stabbed Mr Ratchett to death on the train between Stamboul and Belgrade.

The title instructs us, then, that from the outset the novelist, unlike other kinds of writer, will want to keep the prospective reader in a state of confusion – or, more precisely, 'suspension'. Suspension, that is to say, as in Coleridge's 'suspension of disbelief' ('You will believe a man can fly' or, as in Arthur C. Clarke's 1968 novel *2001: A Space Odyssey*, you will believe that man could have flown to Jupiter *five years ago*). But also 'suspense' in terms of artfully withheld information.

Since most novels tend to be written in the past tense the conclusion must surely be known to the narrator. *Nineteen Eighty-Four*, for example, opens:

> It was a bright cold day in April, and the clocks were striking thirteen. Winston Smith, his chin nuzzled into his breast in an effort to escape the vile wind, slipped quickly through the glass doors of Victory Mansions, though not quickly enough to prevent a swirl of gritty dust from entering along with him.

The narrative 'knows', but will not yet divulge to us the readers, that Winston Smith is destined to rebel against the Party and Big Brother. He will subsequently be captured, tortured, brainwashed – 'hollowed out', as his interrogator O'Brien puts it – and refilled with Party orthodoxy. Citizen 6079, Smith W. will end the novel an exemplary, BB-loving citizen of Oceania. End of story. End of Winston. But the reader, typically, will not be informed of these events until that point when the narrative judges it to be strategically right.

Laurence Olivier's 1948 film of *Hamlet*, conscious that it was serving cultural caviare to the general public, and that the general cinema-going public usually has difficulty with the classics, began with a non-Shakespearian voice-over portentously declaiming: 'This is the story of a man who could not make up his mind.' If *Nineteen Eighty-Four* began with the proclamatory sentence: 'This is the story of a man who rebelled , failed, and ended up with a bullet in the back of his neck' would your reading of Orwell's novel be enhanced, subverted or plain ruined?

The French critic Roland Barthes, in his poststructuralist treatise S/Z, pondered precisely this issue. Novels, he observed, on first reading make artistic use of the 'hermeneutic code' – what the reader does not (yet) know. The pleasure of reading is in not knowing, but then finding out (that is, Colonel Mustard in the Library with the Monkey Wrench). But what, then, of what Barthes called *la deuxième lecture* – the second reading? Cannot *Jane Eyre* still be enjoyed the second, or umpteenth, time you read it and know when, for example, Jane virtuously flees Thornfield to escape Rochester's offer of mistresshood, that she will later on be respectably re-installed in the house as Mrs Rochester? Clearly it is possible to enjoy the novel even though second time round you know what is coming next. Novels, that is, may be designed to be read more than once. It is an assumption most readers are prepared to go along with. Although we may not do it consciously, most readers exercise a kind of triage: novels which, actually or metaphorically, we chuck; and novels which we keep on the shelf to enjoy again, even though we know who killed Colonel Mustard in the Library.

Barthes organised S/Z around a little-known 1830 novella by Balzac called *Sarrasine*. It is a love story, narrated autobiographically. The narrator falls in love at first sight with a stunning young woman at a party. He is sitting on a windowsill (that symbolic threshold between the inner and the outer world). To cut a short story even shorter, in the last paragraph 'she' is revealed to be neither a he nor a she but an it – a castrato. It has the effect, for those not expecting it, of a thunderclap.

Clearly the second reading, when you know what is coming, will be an entirely different experience. You will register, for example, the cunning ambiguity of that window – the transparent membrane between two worlds. Clues, opaque on the first reading, will become clear on the second (such as the repeated window image). Hermeneutically, the narrative will be disabled on second and subsequent readings. Symbolically it may come alive in an even richer way.

Barthes takes an extreme example to make his post-structuralist point. And not every work with a *Sarrasine*-style, smack-you-in-the-face ending will invite revisiting. I do not think Neil Jordan's 1992 film *The Crying Game* works too well second time round, when you know that alarmingly droopy penis is on the way when the knickers come off. I have doubts, too, about Iain Banks's 1984 first novel *The Wasp Factory* (sadistic young castrato who thinks his father has gelded him discovers, in the last section of the narrative, that he has been a normal young she all along). But the *Sarrasine* gimmick is, to whatever extent, embedded in almost all fiction, from mysteries to fables. Fiction without first reading surprise, discovery or revelation is fiction without salt or savour. But there is, for the thoughtful reader, more to fiction than knowing what genitals are beneath the underwear.

I am of an age when many of my friends (as I shall soon, doubtless) have experienced the cruel wear and tear of time. One colleague who had a stroke, but happily recovered, found that, unimpaired as his mind was in a general way, he had lost all sensitivity to nuance. He could not, for example, register irony – it was as if a cat had lost its whiskers, or a bloodhound its sense of smell. Another colleague who suffered a cerebral stroke found that much of his recollection of what novels he had read had been blasted away. His archive was damaged. It was, he said, rather fun re-reading Thomas Hardy and not knowing whether Tess would swing or not. Recovering, that is, the pleasures of *la première lecture*. But, on the whole, the loss of 'field' and depth of reading experience outweighed the individual pleasures of rediscovering novels.

There are no Man Booker or NBA prizes for outstanding titles. But demonstrably some novelists excel over others in this department. Two American masters of the art are Scott Fitzgerald and Ernest Hemingway. Hemingway can, as his story demands, range from the allusively elegiac title (*For Whom the Bell Tolls* (1940) — somebody is going to die), to the ultra-hardboiled (*The Killers* — somebody is going to get murdered) to the biblically portentous (*The Old Man and the Sea* (1952) — somebody is going to spend some time on the cross). Critics concede that even that mid-career clunker, *Across the River and into the Trees* (1950), had a good title. Best stop reading there.

The title of F. Scott Fitzgerald's *The Great Gatsby* (1925) encapsulates the complicated feelings we have about Jay Gatsby — driven by a 'dream', enriched by bootlegging wealth but, for all that (as the narrator Nick insists) 'great'. Would the novel have achieved the near mythic status it now enjoys as, we are told, the most studied work in high schools and colleges across the United States, had Fitzgerald retained one of his original titles, 'Trimalchio in West Egg', or 'The High-Bouncing Lover', or 'Under the Red White and Blue'. Luckily his editor, Maxwell Perkins, argued him out of these 'fatal' suggestions. Nor may the novel have taken off if Perkins had let Fitzgerald call it, Mrs Craik-style, 'James Gatz, Big Shot'. The conclusion? As a general rule it is wise to assume that the titles of novels are not to be trusted. Either they will be duplicitous (saying one thing, meaning others) or they will allude knowingly to works which you, the reader, may not know.

Historically it is possible to locate fairly precisely when the enigmatic, allusive title came on the scene. For it was not always so. Eighteenth-century novels tended to lay out their wares with pedantically explanatory titles. Take the huge

THE
LIFE
AND
STRANGE SURPRIZING
ADVENTURES
OF
ROBINSON CRUSOE,
Of *YORK* Mariner:

Who lived Eight and Twenty Years,
all alone in an un-inhabited Island on the
Coast of AMERICA, near the Mouth of
the Great River of OROONOQUE;

Having been cast on Shore by Shipwreck, where-
in all the Men perished but himself.

WITH

An Account how he was at last as strangely deli-
-ver'd by PYRATES.

Written by Himself.

LONDON;
Printed for W. TAYLOR at the *Ship* in *Pater-Noster-
Row.* MDCCXIX.

An overpacked title page

bill of sale offered for the prospective purchaser of *Robinson Crusoe*:

> The Life and Strange Surprising Adventures of Robinson
> Crusoe of York, Mariner: who lived Eight and Twenty
> Years, all alone in an un-inhabited Island on the coast of
> America, near the Mouth of the Great River of Oroonoque;
> Having been cast on Shore by Shipwreck, wherein all
> the Men perished but himself. With An Account how he
> was at last as strangely deliver'd by Pirates. Written by
> Himself.

Partly this more-than-you-want-to-know on Defoe's part (or, possibly, his printer's) is explained by the primitivism of a genre which had not yet formulated its rules or developed its paratextual machinery. The early eighteenth-century novel did not have available to it all the peripheral information and promotional apparatus of the modern novel: notably, blurbs. First readers of *Robinson Crusoe* needed this grotesquely over-loaded title to set them up and get them into the novel. Partly, too, Defoe's titular surplus relates to how the new novel, as a commodity, was marketed to the public in the eighteenth century. It was normally sold unbound, in 'quires', and the title pages would be hung up, on strings, to attract purchasers. You could not, as you can today, browse: handle the novel, turn to page 69 or, on Amazon, read a sample chapter.

Historically novels were in fairly short supply until well into the nineteenth century. Bibliographies suggest that when Sir Walter Scott and Mrs Ann Radcliffe were the king and queen of the circulating library, around 300 new works of fiction were published annually. This is probably more than anyone (even those scavengers of the circulating library shelves, Isabella Thorpe and Catherine Morland) could actually read – but not the magnitudes more confronting, say, Bridget Jones, who has thirty times that many on offer, and, as a working woman with a full social life, reads fewer.

The crushing surplus of fiction on offer to the middle classes emerged around the middle of the nineteenth century with the industrialisation of the fiction industry and the emergence of the 'leviathan' metropolitan lending libraries – notably, Mudie's and Smith's. Their printed catalogues and advertisers contained thousands of titles, each jostling the others for attention. Florid bindings were one means by which readers were attracted. Illustrated covers (forerunners of the modern dustjacket and paperback cover) were devised, the so-called 'yellowbacks'.

As part of the same project, hyper-enigmatic titles were concocted with which to tickle the jaded library reader's palate: for example, *What will He Do with It?* (Edward Bulwer-Lytton, 1858), *Is He Popenjoy?* (Anthony Trollope, 1878), *Lady Audley's Secret* (Mrs Braddon, 1862). It opened the way to ever more ingenious titles, for those novelists – and there were many – who fancied their skills.

The allusive title emerged about the same period, in the mid nineteenth century. Thackeray's hitting, fortuitously, on the 'exactly right' title for his *magnum opus* is a case in point. For the life stories of Amelia Sedley and Becky Sharp, he originally toyed with two possible titles: 'Pen and Pencil Sketches of English Society' (boring), and 'A Novel without a Hero' (too obviously a sarcastic allusion to Thomas Carlyle's recent lectures on 'Heroes and Hero Worship'). Both were played with on trial title pages, and both remain – archaeologically – as appendages to the final Bunyanesque title. That title, legend has it, came to the author 'unawares in the middle

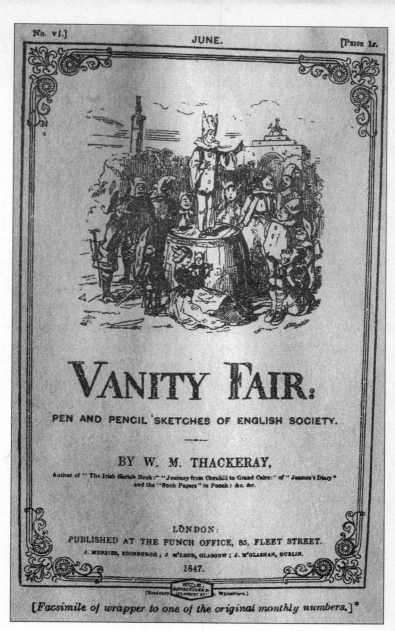

No. vi.]   JUNE.   [Price 1s.

VANITY FAIR:

PEN AND PENCIL SKETCHES OF ENGLISH SOCIETY.

BY W. M. THACKERAY,

Author of " The Irish Sketch Book;" "Journey from Cornhill to Grand Cairo;" of " Jeames's Diary"
and the "Snob Papers" in Punch: &c. &c.

LONDON:
PUBLISHED AT THE PUNCH OFFICE, 85, FLEET STREET.
J. MENZIES, EDINBURGH; J. M'LEOD, GLASGOW; J. M'GLASHAN, DUBLIN.
1847.

[Bradbury &c. &c. Whitefriars.]

[*Facsimile of wrapper to one of the original monthly numbers.*]*

Thackeray mocks Thackeray

of the night' when he was staying at a hotel in Brighton. He 'jumped out of bed and ran three times round his room', uttering as he went, 'Vanity Fair, Vanity Fair, Vanity Fair'.

As Thackeray's bedroom jig exemplifies, it was the perfect title. But the allusion to Bunyan would have been instantly picked up, even by those for whom *Vanity Fair* (1848) was otherwise above their heads. John Bunyan's *The Pilgrim's Progress* (1678) was an eighteenth- and nineteenth-century superseller, particularly with the lower-class reader. Allusions to more remote, or sophisticated, literary sources than Bunyan's homely allegory work in more complicated ways. When for example, Hardy entitled his 1874 novel *Far from the Madding Crowd*, alluding to one of the less hackneyed lines in Thomas Gray's *Elegy Written in a Country Church-yard* (1751)[18] he was, perhaps, countering some critics' unkind portrayal of him as a country bumpkin. He may have been born in Higher Bockhampton, Dorset, the son of a builder. He may have left school at fifteen. But that did not mean that he was an unlettered yokel. There is a touch of the Jude Fawley in the assertive autodidacticism of his choosing to call his Wessex novel *Far from the Madding Crowd* (as in the strange title of another of his novels, *A Laodicean* (1881)). What did the London literary world expect, 'Where the Mangelwurzels Grow'?

Aldous Huxley – Eton, Balliol, most brilliant mind of his generation, with a pedigree that went back to Darwin's bulldog on one side and Dr Arnold on the other – was anything but an autodidact. Even his own name was a literary allusion to the hero of his aunt Mrs Humphry Ward's novel, *Marcella* – no prizes for guessing what Aldous would have been called had he been born a girl. The laboriously highbrow literary echoes in Huxley's titles operate like a kind of snob's Masonic handshake: 'Do you recognise the allusion in the title? If the answer's no, don't bother with this book. It's not for you. Stick to P. C. Wren, my good man.' How do you score on the Aldous Huxley elite reader quiz? (answers are at the end of the chapter):

1. *Antic Hay*
2. *After Many a Summer*
3. *Eyeless in Gaza*
4. *Crome Yellow*
5. *Brave New World*

If you scored more than three, you are permitted to go on to *Ape and Essence*.

There are any number of reasons why some writers 'last' and others, big in their day, do not. Why, for example, has E. F. Benson lasted but not Ivy Compton Burnett? In an April 2006 survey of men's most loved novels, *The Great Gatsby* (1925) made the top five, whereas Theodore Dreiser's *An American Tragedy* (also 1925) came nowhere. In their day, the Jazz Age, the bets would have been preponderantly on Dreiser. Why has he not lasted? Too unjazzy, perhaps?

Huxley too has not, for all his vaunted brilliance, 'lasted' – or, at least, not as well as once seemed likely. Readers are prepared to admire genius, but they dislike novelists who go out of their way make them feel stupid. Allusion still persists in titles and can still be helpful. When, for example, Bret Easton Ellis called his 1991 novel *American Psycho* he intended, I surmise, to travesty such lofty literary compounds as Dreiser's *An American Tragedy* and pay homage to Hitchcock's 1960 film. To know this – or to think that one knows it – is to enhance one's pleasure in Easton's wilfully transgressive fiction. As, for example, does the unliterary, and even more transgressive, allusion in Martin Amis's *Dead Babies*.[19] The conclusion? Don't trust the title. But think about it.

Answers

Answers: 1. 'Antic Hay' is from the sexually depraved Gaveston's opening speech in Christopher Marlowe's *Edward II*, in which Gaveston fantasises about the orgies he, as the King's favourite, will enjoy with the monarch he has corrupted. The antic hay is a dance. 2. 'After many a Summer [Dies the Swan]' is from Tennyson's poem about immortality, *Tithonus*. Having yearned to live for ever, Tithonus now yearns to die. 3. 'Eyeless in Gaza [at the Mill with slaves] is from Milton's *Samson Agonistes*. 4 'Crome Yellow' is not a direct literary allusion, but evokes Oscar Wilde and the scandalous *Yellow Book*. 5. 'Brave New World [that hath such Creatures in it]' is Miranda's ejaculation on seeing human beings other than her father for the first time in her life, in *The Tempest*.

chapter 10

Names

BOOK JACKETS AND COVERS routinely contain four pieces of hard information: 1) the title of the novel; 2) the name of the novelist; 3) the imprint or publisher's identity; 4) the merchandising information packed, illegibly to the human eye, in the bar code. Only the first two matter to the browser–hunter prospective reader. And, as a general rule, with authors' names only one question is worth asking: 'Do I know it?' If the answer is yes, it will have the status of a brand. How strong that brand is expected to be for the general reading public will be reflected in whether it is in larger print on the cover, or dustjacket, than the title of the book. If the author is really 'big', it is giants and pygmies.

All that the title has to do, in such cases, is reassure you the reader that you have not already read it. Whether Stephen King calls his novel *Cujo* (a place? a Native American? a board game?), *Firestarter* (a domestic product all houses should have in winter?) or *Dreamcatcher* (a dozy baseball player?), it doesn't matter. The author name sells the product as effectively as Coca-Cola.

Sometimes other brand names will be introduced a) to endorse and b) to identify a work as being in the same category, or style, as the endorser. King meanz Horror. So when he endorses a work, as he sometimes does, his own brand lends it weight.

If you do not know the author's name, either by direct experience or through word of mouth, the title becomes that much more critical a factor. If you do know the name, previous pleasures, or disappointments, come into play. Walter Scott, for instance, was adamant for the first twelve years (and fifteen novels) of his fiction-writing career that his name should not be printed on his work, nor otherwise divulged. He was 'The Great Unknown'. None the less, his publisher, Archibald Constable, was careful to put prominently on the title page, and in advertisements, 'By the author of *Waverley*' – that being the first, and most explosively bestselling of the series. After a while, of course, the identity of 'The Great Unknown' took on the status of the first great sales gimmick.

Many prospective readers of fiction, on entering a bookshop, do so with the more or less formed intention, 'I want the latest by whoever'. Some will have the intention, probably only vaguely formulated, 'I want something like whoever'. Others will enter, primed with the desire to get a book which is doing well on the bestseller chart, which Richard and Judy, Oprah or someone in their reading group recommended, or which got a rave review from Peter Kemp or Michiko Kakutani in the two great *Times* newspapers.

One thing is certain: an author's name, or pseudonym, and some kind of track record will almost always be required. In the years – roughly mid-1950s to 1980 – when the public library dominated in Britain, readers would experiment with unknown authors because it cost them nothing. It was paid for on the rates – local property taxes. With a six-books-a-fortnight allowance, if a book turned out to be a dud, so what? Take it back and try another; or try another half dozen. But when chancing one's arm on a new author, or an unfamiliar title, costs the best part of twenty quid or thirty bucks, the buyer tends to want reassurance that the cash outlay will not be wasted. That said, one of the few benefits of the British book trade's remorseless '3 for 2' campaigns has been that buyers have been prepared to risk it on the few lucky chosen unknowns. (Not that it is germane here, but the public library era, so to call it, coincided with an unusually innovative phase of British fiction for just this reason: it opened the gates of publication wider than had been historically usual.)

'Anon' was a fashion in the late eighteenth and nineteenth centuries, partly because of the stigma attached to writing fiction as a gentleman's or lady's occupation. Scott turned the whole convention on its head with his Waverley novels. After his blazing career, pseudonymity, rather than anonymity, became the preferred mask. Fiction writing was still, predominantly, a man's world – witnessed by the fact that pseudonymity was routinely utilised as a convenient trans-gendering device – as with 'George Eliot' (Mary Ann Evans), 'Currer, Ellis and Acton Bell' (Charlotte, Emily and Anne Brontë), 'George Egerton' (Mary Chavelita Dunne Bright), 'John Oliver Hobbes' (Pearl Mary Teresa Craigie) and, with an intergendering that Roland Barthes would have relished, Mrs Humphry Ward. Women could, by changing their names, wear the trousers in James's House of Fiction. I know of only one Victorian male who used a female pseudonym, or *alter ego* – William Sharp / Fiona MacLeod.[20]

Pseudonymity is still occasionally used for Victorian motives. The feminist icon Sylvia Plath, for example, published her 1963 novel *The Bell Jar* under the name 'Victoria Lucas' to protect her mother's feelings – similar to the motive that drove Julia Wedgwood, a hundred years earlier, who wrote as 'Florence Dawson' at her father's command. The world, he decreed, should not know a female member of the distinguished and puritanical Wedgwoods (they of the china plate dynasty) had done such as shameful thing as publish a novel. Chamber pots, yes. Father also insisted on editing his daughter's novels: not, it has to be said, to their improvement.

Authors will sometimes use a pseudonym as a means of changing personality: thus Julian Barnes wrote his less than Barnesian 'entertainments', as Greene would have called them, based on Private Eye 'Duffy', under the pseudonym 'Dan Kavanagh' (initially, presumably, a private joke between him and his wife, Pat Kavanagh). Iain Banks writes realism under that name and science fiction under the slightly pseudonymised Iain M. Banks. One of the more ingenious uses of modern pseudonym is that of Stephen King who, when it seemed that he was flooding the market, started varying his product under the pseudonym Richard Bachman ('back man'). When the ruse was tumbled by his fans, King arranged for his alter ego to die by 'cancer of the pseudonym' – but not before a couple of unpublished Bachman novels were found in the attic.

Clearly, if the reader is to wring the most out of a pseudonymised work it helps to know the author's real identity behind the mask. It is not, however, always possible. No one out of the millions who have seen the 1948 classic movie *Treasure of the Sierra Madre* and gone on to read the novel can, to this day, be sure of the identity of its author, 'B. Traven' – best guess is he may have been a German anarchist, Ret Marut. It adds a lustre to the story. During his lifetime, no one could work out who the mystery writer 'Trevanian' was. The author of the novel on which that other much re-run 1972 movie *The Eiger Sanction* is based, Trevanian was revealed, long after the event, to be a professor of communications from Texas, Rodney Whitaker. It would not have added much lustre to the thriller.

Pseudonymity still flourishes, if it is not as widespread as in the nineteenth century, and most energetically in genre, pulp and graphic fiction (a field in which untangling author-ship is particularly tricky), where it often masks embarrassing overproduction on the author's part. Anonymity, by contrast, is used nowadays only as a gimmick. When *Primary Colors*, the 1996 tell-all *roman à clef* about the Clintons' rocky road from Arkansas to the White House, came out it was advertised as having been written by 'Anon' – an insider, we were led to believe, for whom it would be dangerous to be identified, the Deep Throat of fiction. It was only after forensic examination by the FBI's house stylometrician, Professor Don Foster, that Anon was identified as the journalist Joe Klein. He was indeed an insider, although whether the incognito gimmick was really necessary is a moot point.

The mystery was exploited, very effectively, by *Primary Colors*' publisher to whet the public appetite. Such 'Who is Anon?' gimmicks can be traced all the way back to London publisher Henry Colburn, the 'Prince of Puffers', as he was nicknamed in the 1820s for his outrageous advertising stunts. Colburn regularly marketed his 'silver fork' fiction (that is, novels about fashionable life) as being by 'eminent hands' – but hands which could not, for obvious reasons, be identi-fied. What would their friends in high places think? Authorial names, it would seem, can, like titles, play games with the reader. They add to the fun.

chapter 11

Worth a thousand words

TITLES AND AUTHORS' names are self-evidently things of words. Nowadays novels are routinely embellished, on the hardback dustjacket, and slightly less often on the paperback cover, by a 'publicity photo' of the author – something which is viewed rather than read. Obviously what the novelist looks like is unimportant in forming any critical opinion of the novel. But, like much of the peripheral apparatus which the booktrade has shrewdly devised and perfected over the years, it has a palpable effect on the reading experience. More so as the photograph is, typically, 'framed' by readers' perceptions of what it is, at this point in time, to be an author. Such perceptions change over time.

Novelists of the nineteenth century first began to use publicity photographs in the great *carte de visite* mania of the 1860s, when photography for the masses became a viable proposition. It also, as literary historians have recorded, changed the canons of narrative realism; as did the arrival of film, forty years later.[21] In the middle of the twentieth century

The 'Great Inimitable', the creator of Philip
Marlowe, and the contemporary crusader

studio photos of the author embellished novels (by Yousuf
Karsh, or Cecil Beaton, if the novelist warranted it). Publicity
photographs, as with everything else, have loosened up in the
last fifty years. It would be possible to write a history of the
novel in terms of the poses which novelists have struck for
the lens over the last century and a half, and the changing
iconography of authorship those poses project.

What do the above images convey, authorially? The Victorian sage; the cigarette-smoking, tweed-wearing bookman;
the beautiful fighter for human rights, a La Pasionara of the
Green movement. The 'semiotics' (what am I signalling to you
by my appearance) are historically different and – for those
with a curious eye – register the changing image of what this
novelist is, beyond a neutral tale teller. Practice has changed
over the years. For several decades, for example, Penguin
editions of the ageing Evelyn Waugh's and Iris Murdoch's
novels had cover photographs taken in the authors' salad
days. The current practice is for contemporaneity.

One of the more useful pieces of advice given to examination students is, when answering the question, to visualise, in

as much detail as you can, the examiner you are writing for: as a person you are conversing with, that is, not a veiled, Delphic figure who holds your destiny in her/his hand. So, too, with novels. Without making the crass error of confusing narrator and author (Holden Caulfield is not J. D. Salinger) the novelist is always there in the novel – if only as the ghost in the text. It is a plus to be able to put a face to the name. How different *Middlemarch* would be, for example, if you were to read it under the misapprehension that it was written by a pipe-smoking Victorian clubman called George Eliot. Imagine if *From Russia with Love* (1957) were embellished not with this photograph of the suave Ian Fleming, but some sad old codger like E. Phillips Oppenheim (the Fleming of his day).

Sometimes, however, it is not possible to lodge an image of the author in the mind, as you read. The Walter Scott of our day is Thomas Pynchon, of whom no authenticated photograph exists.[22] Even the class mugshot of him at his *alma mater*, Cornell, has, apparently, been removed from the record. He is the Great Unphotographable. The unusualness adds to the zest of reading, say, *Gravity's Rainbow*.

chapter 12

Famous first words

THE PROSPECTIVE READER has, then, a number of initial 'encounters', so to speak, with the novel before she reads it. Reviews and word of mouth may form a distant introduction. The first sight of the cover and the title are other early encounters. A quick-read scan of the blurb and shoutlines on the jacket form another. Some cursory examination of the prelims represents an encounter of the fourth kind.

But the first 'close' encounter will be the first line of the text. This is the moment of coupling. The following are two of the more famous first lines, or sentences, in fiction: they are much quoted and will be found in all self-respecting anthologies of quotation as stand-alone statements about the human condition:

All happy families are alike. All unhappy families are unhappy in their own way.

It is a truth universally acknowledged, that a single man in possession of a good fortune must be in want of a wife.

The first is from Tolstoy's *Anna Karenina*: the second from Jane Austen's *Pride and Prejudice*. Neither assertion is at all plausible, outside the socially artificial world which the novelist has created and into which the sentences usher us. They are, in more than one sense, fictional. Thomas Harris's 1988 bestseller *The Silence of the Lambs*, for example, could have opened with the lofty proposition: 'It is a truth universally acknowledged that every psychotherapist, of advanced intellectual capacity, is in want of a human liver to eat with fava beans and a big Amarone.' It is not, even in the little world of Longbourn, true that every single man in possession of a fortune, etc., must be in search of a wife. Bingley may be; Darcy certainly is not. He seems, if anything, to be infused with misogynistic Byronism. What is his first comment on Miss Bennet at the Meryton ball? 'She is tolerable; but not handsome enough to tempt me; and I am in no humour at present to give consequence to young ladies who are slighted by other men.' (Swine.) These are scarcely the words of a man with a fortune in search of a wife. They indicate, rather, a rich man well aware that the mothers of England are stalking him. What the apparently universal truth at the opening of the novel lays down are the distorted parameters within which a free spirit like Elizabeth Bennet is obliged to operate – and a wholly mercenary spirit like Mrs Bennet is all too happy to operate.

So, too, with the Tolstoy. It is manifestly not true that there is only one kind of family happiness. Is the happiness of the Vicar of Wakefield's domestic circle the same as that tentative happiness reached by the hero and heroine at the conclusion of Ian McEwan's 1997 novel *Enduring Love*? What Tolstoy's pseudo-pontifical 'truism' sets up is the large question hovering over the life choices that Anna makes. Would she have been happier had she accepted her bourgeois, limited existence and the compromised happiness it guaranteed? Or is she justified in yearning, and reaching for, something larger, with all the attendant risks? Would it really have been a happy-ever-after had she never returned to Moscow and Vronsky? Had she, that is, embraced the destiny of a respectable wife and mother? Is not 'happy family', in Tolstoy's world, as created in *Anna Karenina*, a contradiction in terms? Within the novels these overarching statements – which echo, more or less ironically, until the last page – create a climate, or rule of life, within which the narrative operates. They put the reader on the track. They are not, to echo Austen, universal truths.

Consider next another famous first sentence:

Call me Ishmael.

Like Proust's redolent madeleine or the first line of *Finnegans Wake* ('riverrun, past Eve and Adam's ...'), 'Call me Ishmael' is proverbial, known even to those who would not know Herman Melville's 1851 masterpiece *Moby-Dick* from the spotted variety served up as dessert. It has been the subject of innumerable jokes. That by Peter de Vries (a sadly forgotten comic novelist), through the sly interjection of a comma, creates the kind of travesty which would appeal to Lynne Truss:

Call me, Ishmael.

As in, that is, 'ET, your mother's waiting for a phone call from you on Tralfamadore'.

Far from putting the reader on the track, however, Melville's first line sets us on a very bumpy course. The hero narrator's name is, it appears, not Ishmael (but you can call me that). As the notes of the student editions inform us, the *nom de plume* is freighted with allegorical significance – but who, under his Biblical name of convenience, is this 'Ishmael'? He is, it seems, suffering from some kind of depression and is going to sea as a kind of therapy – the sailing cure (beats Prozac). He is clearly very literate: far more literate, as the encyclopaedic chapters on cetology witness, than most able-bodied seamen. There is a hint, in chapter 11, that he has had an unhappy childhood and was mistreated by his mother. But at the end of an immensely long narrative we know less about his life before joining the *Pequod* than about its captain Ahab's wife and children (another black hole in the text). Why does Melville play these games with us? Even the whale has a proper name. Why not Ishmael? Why this vagueness in a novel which goes into much more detail than we want to know about the sexual equipment of the sperm whale (its 'cassock', or silky scrotum sack, for example). The first line of *Moby-Dick* hangs, like an unresolved question mark, over the 1000 pages of text, tincturing it with enigma.

In any competition for the ten most resonant first sentences in fiction I would, among all the other usual suspects (best of times, worst of times; clocks striking thirteen; dark and stormy nights, riverrun, the past as foreign country, etc.) give a prominent place to 'Last night I dreamed I went to Manderley again'. For those not familiar with Daphne Du Maurier's *Rebecca* (1938), the remark is tantalising. Is Manderley a place? A town? An estate? A great house? An imaginary country? Why the stress on 'again'? Can Manderley, whatever it may be, not be revisited in the flesh? Who is 'I'?

As the novel unfolds, the enigma dissolves, with one exception. We never learn either the first name or the maiden name of 'I', even though she is even more important than her predecessor as Mrs de Winter, Rebecca, in the narrative. Artfully, Du Maurier keeps that information as withheld to the last sentence as it was in the first. It creates an unusual effect which, doubtless, has contributed to the perennial appeal of Du Maurier's romance.

Demonstrably, novelists who care take huge care with the opening words of their works. In Camus' 1947 fictional allegory of the Nazi Occupation, La Peste (The Plague) there is a would-be novelist who, with ultra-Flaubertian scrupulosity, wrestles interminably over the first line of his magnum opus. But he can never perfect it, so the novel is for ever blocked. It is a joke, but it contains a proverbial truth. Even the longest novel has to begin with a single line, and that line sets the narrative on the path to its destination.

First lines, then, should never be taken at face value. But if you are applying the sniff test in the shop, the first line is always worth a quick dab at the nostrils. Best not do it with last lines as the-butler-did-it style revelations are likely to spoil your first reading.

chapter 13

Epigraphs, forewords and afterwords

SWIFT CALLED THE opening pages to a book 'the great doorway'. Sneaks, he complained, snuck in the back way, via the index (or, if you are reading a detective novel, by the-butler-did-it last page). One of the side entrances, to be found in Henry James's House of Fiction, is the epigraph. This conventionally has the honour of a page to itself – a non-trivial production cost in some periods of book history. (You can generally gauge the current price of paper by the 'solidity' of the type – the vast white pages and generous 'leading' in the Victorian three-decker was made possible by the arrival of cheap, industrially produced paper in the early nineteenth century.)

Not all novels have epigraphs – it is an optional extra, unlike the title page. Where epigraphs are to be found, they are invariably worth looking at. Take, for example, one of the epigraphs to Zadie Smith's 2005 Man Booker prize short-listed *On Beauty*:

> To misstate, or even merely understate, the relation of
> the universities to beauty is one kind of error that can
> be made. A university is among the precious things that
> can be destroyed.
>
> *Elaine Scarry*

The quotation is from Scarry's 1999 treatise on aesthetics and immorality, *On Beauty and being Just*. Thematically appropriate, given that Smith's novel is about art history and immorality on an American campus, the epigraph works in other ways. Elaine Scarry is an English professor at Harvard, where Smith spent the years preceding the publication of her novel. Scarry is, unlike most of her ivory-tower-bound profession, an academic with interests far outside her discipline (in the causation of recent air crashes, for example, about which she has interestingly unofficial theories). Her treatise *On Beauty and being Just* argues for the necessity of aesthetics and its union with the 'real world' from which, like *objets d'art* in a museum, it is traditionally fenced off.

In Smith's acknowledgements to her novel (prepended in *On Beauty* – where they are found in fiction they are usually appended), she declares roundly that 'It should be obvious that this is a novel inspired by a love of E. M. Forster, to whom all my fiction is indebted, one way or the other. This time I wanted to repay the debt with *hommage*.' As most reviewers and many readers instantly recognise, the novel opens with an unmistakeable echo of the opening of Forster's 1910 novel *Howards End*: 'One may as well begin with ...' It is also worth considering the epigraph to Forster's novel – 'only connect'.

The main action of *On Beauty* is set in an American university on the eastern seaboard. On the face of it the narrative is as disconnected from Forster's Bloomsbury as from Mars.

Smith's novel, at its outset, deals with the fraught relationship of two art historians, one worldly, one donnish. Their
families are, in terms of pigmentation and culture, 'blended'
– the constituents ranging from Rembrandt to Tupac Shakur.
Again there would seem to be no connection with the serene,
soon to be shattered, Edwardian Englishness of *Howards End*.
But clearly Smith is signalling to us that deep connections
are present, even if we are not immediately aware of them.
Novels, particularly novels as complex as *On Beauty*, are not
to be boiled down and packaged, like sugar, as cubes of easily
absorbed 'meaning'. But Smith's novel, as signalled by its
epigraph, is centrally interested in 'connection' – across the
Atlantic, across race and, as in Forster, between the world of
art (aesthetics) and the world of 'telegrams and anger' (or
aircraft crashes), across class, and between the youngest,
post-colonial flowering of English (and more than English)
fiction and the author of *A Passage to India*.

The 'blendedness', to paraphrase Forster's 'only connect',
can even be seen in the author's photograph in *On Beauty* – a
paratextual peripheral missing from the dustjacket of the
1910 edition of *Howards End*. Recall the ending of *A Passage
to India* (1924), with the two men – whom we may with only
a little fancifulness see as lovers, separated by each other's
cultures: 'Why can't we be friends now?' asks the British
Fielding, holding the Muslim Aziz. 'It's what I want. It's what
you want.'

But the horses didn't want it – they swerved apart; the
earth didn't want it, sending up rocks through which
riders must pass single file; the temples, the tank, the jail,
the palace, the birds, the carrion, the Guest House, that
came into view as they issued from the gap and saw Mau

beneath; they didn't want it, they said in their hundred voices, 'No, not yet,' and the sky said, 'No, not there.'

Zadie Smith, the triumphantly English but racially blended author, would seem, physically, to incarnate that deferred connection which, for Forster in 1924, was in the far future. (In 1924, Smith, aged twenty-five when she published her first novel *White Teeth* (2000), being a woman under the age of twenty-eight, would not have been allowed to vote although by the time of *On Beauty*'s publication, she was an enfranchised 29-year-old).

Can a reader appreciate *On Beauty* without the connected epigraphic baggage? Yes, but it adds to that appreciation. Very often the epigraph to a novel, where it exists, will encapsulate the essence less hucksterishly than the blurb, and more directly than the title. Greene's 1948 novel about altruistic suicide (a mortal sin?), *The Heart of the Matter*, has a typically riddling title. But the epigraph, from the French Catholic essayist Charles Péguy, sums up the central moral paradox in the novel with crystalline clarity: 'The sinner is at the very heart of Christianity ... No one is as competent as the sinner in Christian affairs. No one, except the Saint.' And which of those is the hero, Scobie?

So, look at the epigraph before investing in a novel. It is sometimes worth the second or so it takes. It is also worth pondering dedications. They tend to be private, but can sometimes illuminate. That to *On Beauty*, for example, is to Zadie Smith's husband, Nick Laird, one of whose love poems (to the author) is integrated into the text. David Lodge's dedication in his 1965 university campus novel *The British Museum is Falling Down* points to another interesting side door: 'To Malcolm Bradbury (whose fault it mostly is that I have tried to write a comic novel)'. For novels, their authors remind us, typically converse with each other. Lodge and Bradbury's twin careers in British campus fiction clearly played off each other – so much so that someone came up with the proposition that they were one novelist, Bradlodge (or 'Blodge', as the more rueful Birmingham novelist put it). The conversation is rarely as audible as it is here and we must be grateful to the dedication for cueing us. It enriches our appreciation of both novelists.

chapter 14

Read one, you've read them all: intertextuality

THE PRECEDING THOUGHTS about 'connectedness' lead to a related consideration. When you read *The British Museum is Falling Down* or *On Beauty* you are not reading merely a 'novel', but 'fiction'. No novel, that is to say, is a literary island, entire of itself. It is to Julia Kristeva, the French theorist, that we owe the useful term 'intertextuality'.[23] We should resist, she suggests, the temptation to see works of literature as separate objects, like so many green bottles standing on the literary wall. Fiction is more in the nature of a great web, echo chamber or cultural ensemble, in which every novel, however faintly, reverberates with every other novel.

Kristeva is that dreaded thing, a foreign literary theorist who writes fiction on the side. Her 2006 novel *Murder in Byzantium* illustrates her intertextuality thesis admirably, being a blend (not entirely without its lumps) of *crime noir*, *The Name of the Rose* (leavened with touches of Indiana Jones) and *The Silence of the Lambs*, featuring as it does a serial murderer called, enigmatically, 'No. 8' – a name more appropriate to one of his luckless victims, perhaps.

If it veers too close, intertextuality shades into either *hommage* (as in, say, Terry Southern's 1958 novel *Candy* and Voltaire's *Candide* – the sexual progress of an *ingénue* and *ingénu* respectively) or downright plagiarism. Sometimes, without an author being aware of it, another author's text will infect the work in progress: 'cryptomnesia', as it is called – unconscious theft. The distinctions are examined scrupulously by the German critic Michael Maar in his 2005 monograph *The Two Lolitas*. Did Nabokov know – did he misappropriate? – his famous work from a short story called 'Lolita' by the German author Heinz von Lichberg? Whether he did or he did not, neither would be unusual in the world of fiction.

Kristeva's intertextuality thesis which, like the best such theses, merely labels something already intuitively known, can again be tested with reference to titles shortlisted for the Man Booker prize in 2005 – novels, on the face of them, of the highest originality, as distinct from each other as their authors.

Zadie Smith, a product of the Cambridge literature school – once the refuge of E. M. Forster, later the hotbed of Brito-Gallic literary theory – is, as noted in the previous section, overt in paying her intertextual dues. Her novel opens with a replication of the opening of *Howards End* which in any discourse other than literature would look like plagiarism, or gross copycatism:

One may as well begin with Jerome's e-mails to his father.
One may as well begin with Helen's letters to her sister.

In *Howards End*, the letter which Helen sends her sister Margaret reports her having fallen impulsively in love with Paul, the son of the worldly Wilcox family. In *On Beauty*, the parallel email reports Jerome Belsey having fallen impulsively in love with the daughter of the worldly Kipps family. In neither case does it work out. The stressed similarities continue throughout the narratives – rather too heavy handedly for some reviewers of Smith's novel. What she intended, perhaps, was to keep in the reader's mind the fact that hers is a novel not merely in a tradition, but in direct engagement with other novels in that tradition.

Although *On Beauty* had its strong supporters on the judging committee (myself among others), *The Sea* won the Man Booker prize. In Banville's novel intertextuality is blatantly proclaimed with the elemental title. There are innumerable other novels with similar (identically in some instances) titles – including one former winner of the Booker Prize, Iris Murdoch's *The Sea, the Sea* (1978). *The Sea*, true to its title, opens with a description of just that:

> The seabirds mewled and swooped, unnerved, it seemed, by the spectacle of that vast bowl of water bulging like a blister, lead-blue and malignantly agleam. They looked unnaturally white, that day, those birds. The waves were depositing a fringe of soiled yellow foam along the waterline.

If, to paraphrase Coleridge, you had met those lines wandering wild in Arabia you would have shouted 'Joyce' – specifically the description of the sea off Dublin a few paragraphs into *Ulysses* (1922):

God!, he said quietly. Isn't the sea what Algy calls it: a great sweet mother? The snotgreen sea. The scrotum-tightening sea. *Epi oinopa ponton.* Ah, Dedalus, the Greeks! I must teach you. You must read them in the original. *Thalatta! Thalatta!* She is our great sweet mother. Come and look.

Joyce, whose title is no more original than Banville's, is picking up on the Homeric (and very odd, chromatically) 'wine-dark sea' in *The Odyssey*. The three sentences are, of course, thick as custard with allusiveness. 'Algy', for example, is Algernon Swinburne, and the reference is to his poem 'The Triumph of Time'. Dedalus, the surname of the young hero of the book, makes almost too obvious a reference to Greek myth. (Is anyone, in the length and breadth of Ireland, surnamed Dedalus? As likely as 'Paddy Hercules'.) *Thalatta! Thalatta!* – 'The sea, the sea' – is what the remnant of Xenophon's troops cry out in his *Anabasis* when they catch a glimpse of the Black Sea, after their escape from Babylon. This is, it may be recalled, also the titular allusion in Iris Murdoch's Booker-winning novel. And why scrotumtightening? Unlike the Aegean, the Atlantic is cold and does drastic things to a man's testicles.

Banville, of course, is a great Irish novelist. He is, inter-textually, paying his dues. The function of the intertextual gesture is a kind of deference. There are other, more struc-tural connections. Banville's hero, Max Morden, is a Leopold Bloom AD 2005 – fatalistic, in the dead end of a marriage (more literally than Bloom), gloomily meditative about the human condition. But, as Banville conceives him, gloomily eloquent as well.

A third shortlist contender in 2005, *The Accidental* by Ali

Smith, tells the story, with remarkable narrative obliquity, of a family of our time, the Flints (a slyly invisible suffix '-stones' hovers). The father is an English lecturer who cannot, as they say in academic circles, keep his dick inside his pants and outside the students'. The mother is a 'counterfactual' historian, a writer of 'real' fictions. The Flints have two precocious, hypersensitive and troubled children. Smith's narrative flits artfully between the various centres of consciousness, charting the family's quiet, but very eloquent desperation, as a set of glinting interior monologues.

The family has its stress points, but it is holding together – just. Its fragile cohesion is unglued beyond repair by the arrival of a mysterious and beautiful stranger, Amber. Amber may or may not be supernatural. Her effect, accompanied by rampant seduction, is somehow to supercharge the break-up of the family – but eventually to drive it to a new formation which is less comfortably bourgeois, but more honest.

Amber is 'accidental'; not written in any sense into the 2005 middle-class life script. The intertextual connection, as a number of reviewers and readers apprehended, is with Pasolini's 1968 film *Theorema*, in which a mysterious, beautiful stranger, played by Terence Stamp, arrives from nowhere into a family and, simply by virtue of what he is, destroys their merely 'theoretic' coherence.

Smith's novel is manifestly as much intergeneric as it is intertextual. The filmic connection is stressed in the CV of Amber, which presents her as the offspring of cinema – an image, not a person:

> He had sat opposite her at supper. She looked the kind of girl, no, the kind of good full adult woman, that you'd pick up in a car on the road and give a lift to the next

village, then she'd get out of your car and wave goodbye and you'd never see her again, but you'd never forget it.

She looked like the dishevelled, flower-strewn girl in Botticelli's *Spring*.

He had got off the train surprised at himself. He had stood for a moment in the sun. He had stood watching simple sunlight glinting off his car in the station car park. He had felt strange, different, shiny under his clothes, so much so that on his way home he had begun to think he should maybe take an antihistamine. When he got home the Volvo was still in the drive. He parked his car alongside it. He walked round the side of the house. She was lying on her front in the garden examining something, like a girl. When he saw her his heart was a wing in the air.

He had made supper. He had made an excellent supper. Is she staying for supper? he'd asked Eve when she came in. I've no idea, Eve said, have you asked her to?

Julian Barnes's *Arthur and George*, our fourth novel in the 2005 Man Booker set, deals, docufictionally, with an actual episode in the life of Arthur Conan Doyle. Late in his career, and by now world famous as the creator of Sherlock Holmes, Doyle was asked to help an obscure solicitor, George Edjali, a wholly anglicised Parsi who had been framed, and ruined professionally, on a trumped-up charge of cattle mutilation. Barnes, the most Francophile of British novelists, is clearly playing off Zola's famous 1898 broadside against the French government for its handling of the Dreyfus affair *J'accuse*. In a minor, Anglo-Saxon key, Edjali's persecution was a Dreyfus scandal this side of the channel. But as artfully Barnes (who, as I have previously mentioned, also writes detective novels as 'Dan Kavanagh') also plays off the Sherlock Holmes narrative routines in which the omniscient amateur sleuth, like some chess grandmaster, moves with effortless and infallible virtuosity to the solution of his case.

In life, although he got Edjali off, Doyle made the most horrendous blunder as regards the key piece of evidence. He discovered the lancet with which the crimes were committed but stole it – thus tainting the article, so that it could never be admitted in court. What he perpetrated was less 'The Case of the Silk Stocking' than 'The Case of the Bodged Lancet'. Real-life sleuthing, Barnes's novel seems to aver (something enhanced by its pseudo-factuality), is no profession for amateurs. Leave that to the 'novel'.

It would be possible to pursue this theme on intertextuality with all the novels on the Man Booker list, probably any of the thousands of novels published in 2005. But it is unnecessary. The fact is novels all connect at some level and in some way – however subterranean that connection. The more intriguing question is: supposing you have not read, say, or do not even know of the existence of *Howards End*, *Ulysses*, Sherlock Holmes or Pasolini's films – would these four novels be inaccessible? How necessary, for enjoyment and full appreciation, is it to recognise the intertextual connections that link a novel to other novels?

For enjoyment, not very necessary. George MacDonald Fraser's *Flashman* novels are, for example, a massive and protracted intertextual jape, taking off from Thomas Hughes's 1857 novel of life in a boys' public school, *Tom Brown's Schooldays*. That novel, as well known in the first half of the twentieth century as Sir Robert Baden-Powell's *Rovering to Success* (1930), is little read today. And it is almost entirely unread in America where 'public school' has a quite different connotation from Eton, Rugby, Harrow and 'Play up, play up and play the game'.

Many Americans, famously, correspond with Fraser assuming that Flashy is an actual historical personage. None the less, even without the slightest knowledge of Hughes's work to bounce off, the Flashman novels are clearly enjoyed. Perhaps, on the ignorance is bliss principle, even better enjoyed. The most lively fan-based Flashman websites are located in the United States.

You do not have to understand all the internal wiring of a novel to enjoy the illumination it gives. But being aware of it does give the reader a pleasing sense of ascendancy, and of almost egalitarian connection with the author. In conclusion, for the 'user' the message is simple. The more fiction you read, and the more intelligently you do so, the richer your experience will be. Those readers who read most get most out of it.

chapter 15

On the rack: know your genre

'LET YOUR FINGERS do the walking', the advertisements for the business telephone directory the *Yellow Pages*
used to advise. That is also the implicit inducement offered
by the electronic webstores which, increasingly, are the
fiction reader's first port of call – as, thirty years ago, was the
public library; and, thirty years before that, the cornershop
'tuppenny libraries' and, fifty years before that, the 'circulating libraries' and, a century before that, the 'colporteurs'
or itinerant pedlars.

Things get ever more convenient for the fiction reader (but
not, for that reason, necessarily easier). You can, for example,
read a strong review of a novel in an online newspaper, or
register its presence on the just-released *Times* bestseller
list and, with a few clicks, order the same work, healthily
discounted, from Amazon or www.whoeverelse.com for next
morning delivery, without stirring your stumps from the
chair. Hemiplegic shopping.

Bookshops, requiring as they do the use of eyes, legs

and hands, still have an advantage in one respect – their physical layout. Most large bookstores are compartmentalised – and, within the general category 'fiction', novels are further sorted. 'Romance and gothic' will, disproportionately (although not entirely), attract women readers. Their male counterparts will, generally, find their way to 'male action', science fiction and – preponderantly, but not overwhelmingly so – crime (why? Look at the population of the nation's prisons). Although, following on their pioneer 'cosy crime' predecessors, Agatha Christie and Dorothy L. Sayers, contemporary writers like Patricia Cornwell, Sue Grafton and Sara Paretsky have made this area less of a male preserve than it once was. Gays will go proudly to their annex. Smut hounds will slink to erotica. But with the arrival of crossover lines such as Richard Branson's (yes) Black Lace (Mills and Boon without the chastity knickers), segregation is crumbling even in that naughty corner of the bookshop. Students, if they are dutiful, and retired school teachers gravitate to the classic reprint shelves. George Eliot here we come. Horror is often mixed in with sf and fantasy. Writers like V. C. Andrews and Dean Koontz, I suspect, have gender-specific constituencies, but their titles will be found nestling alongside each other, like vampire bats in a cave.

Genre differentiation offers a useful and easily handled geography of fiction – something that allows readers to find their bearings, to choose within the known area of novels they prefer, or are curious about, and avoid those that do nothing for them. Few middle-aged men of decent moral character will find themselves in teen fiction. Not many teenagers, I suspect, buy Andy McNab and the other SAS warrior scribes who have found the pen, if not mightier than the SA80, then substantially more profitable. Pity the country, said Brecht, which needs heroes; or, I might add, novels about heroes by Sergeant McNab.

Legs, where books are concerned, can walk you to what you want more efficiently than fingers. The webstores, for all their techno frills, are very poor at mapping and serving up genre. Their automated search engines, for example, find it difficult to separate J. G. Ballard's non-sf *Empire of the Sun* (1984) from the bulk of his work, which is science fiction. There are no machine-readable mark-ups in the titles, or the ISBNs, to indicate the genre family to which Ballard's separate works of fiction belong. So too with, say, John Grisham. Electronic browsing does not separate his cute *Skipping Christmas* (2001) from his hallmark legal thrillers. Bookstore staff can handle such separations with no trouble whatsoever. Ballard's *The Drowned World* (1962) is dispatched to 'sf and fantasy', *Empire of the Sun* and *Cocaine Nights* (1996) to general fiction.

The evolution of genre is a late development in the long history of fiction – a kind of branching from the main trunk line once it had driven down its literary roots. There are, loosely speaking, four main genres: women's romance; sf; horror and fantasy; male action/thriller/western; crime. From these branching genres, there are further offshoots – subgenres, or genres within genres (e.g. chicklit, ladlit, weepies, creepies, shopping and fucking, docuthrillers). Genre is one of the least static of fictional domains. It is always branching out – faster than the trade can name it, often.

Historically, if you return to the origins and the 'rise of the novel' era, you can identify Samuel Richardson's *Pamela* (1740) as proto-chicklit (as an American student once described it to me). *Robinson Crusoe* is proto-male action. Jonathan Swift's *Gulliver's Travels* (1726) is proto-sf. The kernels of genre are there from the beginning. It is conventional to date

detective fiction from William Godwin's *Caleb Williams* (1794)
– although the Blifil subplot of *Tom Jones* (1749) is a detective
story *avant la lettre*, relying as it does on evidence and clues
on the way to denouement. (Who purloined the letter? The
wicked stepbrother. Elementary, my dear Caleb.)

But the precise generic territories, formats, styles and
conventions of what we now know as genre – the rules of the
game(s) – had not been definitively charted in the eighteenth
century and would not be until a hundred years later: a period
in which distinct starting points can be located. It was the
American dime novel which laid down the blueprint for the
western. The first such, *Malaeska*, came out in 1860. Interestingly, it was written by a woman, Ann S. Stephens. Calamity
Jane, a female, chap-wearing, chap-kicking gunslinger, was
also an early series heroine riding the dime novel range. These
novels, close as they were to the pioneer life in the west, are
probably truer to historical fact than their direct descendant,
Hollywood's generic, twentieth-century western, with its
subordinated little women, primly preparing the evening
chow for their men.

The detective novel, in its modern form, is usually dated
from Edgar Allan Poe's 'locked room mystery' 'The Murder
in the Rue Morgue' (1841), 'The Purloined Letter' (1844) and
his omniscient sleuth, Auguste Dupin (ancestor of Poirot and
Scarpetta – there is a recurrent fondness in detective fiction
for deuced clever foreign detectives). Poe can claim to be a
founding genius of genre. His stories explore the possibilities
of horror, the detective novel and the gothic romance. Poe's
originality (he burned out in a welter of alcoholic dissipa-
tion, aged barely forty) was celebrated by the genius of Roger
Corman, in the late twentieth century, with a string of low-
budget, high camp masterpieces (many featuring Vincent

Price, ham *extraordinaire*) which paid homage to the author's extraordinary inventiveness.

As regards detective fiction the prime British contender is Wilkie Collins's *The Moonstone* (1868), whose Sergeant Cuff of Scotland Yard is the ancestor of Inspector Morse and whole brigades of other plain clothes police detectives. Collins's novel, however, like its even more popular predecessor, *The Woman in White* (1860) belongs centrally to the Victorians' beloved 'sensation novel' genre. Prior claim can also be made for Inspector Bucket in *Bleak House* (1853), although that officer (based on Dickens's admired 'thieftaker' Inspector Field) is confined to subplot status. *Bleak House* is social problem fiction (another favourite, if less fun, Victorian genre) with a detective story in the background.

The 1890s, and Sherlock Holmes's sensational entry into the pages of Newnes's *Strand Magazine*, with its Sidney Paget illustrations (he it was who invented the trademark deerstalker), gave detective fiction its greatest boost. So successful was Holmes that not even the combined forces of Moriarty and his own creator, Conan Doyle, could kill him. Back he came to tame the Baskerville hound, wired up on his 7 per cent solution.

Spy fiction originates with the sensational fictions of William Le Queux, such as *A Secret Service* (1896); although the most influential predecessor of Smiley and Harry Palmer is Erskine Childers's *The Riddle of the Sands* (1903). The secret agent (007) offshoot is conventionally seen to emerge in its mature form with W. Somerset Maugham's First World War stories in *Ashenden* (1928), and the formation of the Ministries of Intelligence (MI5 and MI6) as responses to the twentieth century's hot and cold wars.

The pedigree of science fiction is contentious – tangled

as it is in antique fable, allegory and utopian fiction. Some, like Brian Aldiss (himself a distinguished practitioner) would take as the genre's starting point Mary Shelley's *Frankenstein* (1818) – a novel in which science refashions natural creation, disastrously. Another suggestion is Colonel Chesney's 1871 'invasion fantasy', inspired by the fall of Paris in the Franco-Prussian war, *The Battle of Dorking*. Chesney's novella was such a runaway success at the time, and so terrifying, that Gladstone himself was obliged to warn the population against 'alarmism' (as, a century and a half later, did the Bush administration in the face of the alarm generated by Roland Emmerich's 2004 climate change catastrophe movie, *The Day after Tomorrow*). *The Battle of Dorking* is the clear inspiration for H. G. Wells's and, more recently, Steven Spielberg's *The War of the Worlds*. Like many genres, sf has a strong vein of paranoia running through it. It is no accident that it boomed in the early twentieth century with immigration panics in the UK and the US and the 1905 Aliens Registration Act. Or that Spielberg's 2005 movie version ('The Greatest Action Epic Ever', as it was advertised) coincided with collective hysteria about the Al Qaeda enemy within.

Another sf pioneer, and my personal favourite by virtue of its sheer zaniness, is Bulwer-Lytton's *The Coming Race*, written in 1871 – an *annus mirabilis* for sf. The novel is innovative enough to merit a brief summary. Lytton's hero is a bumptious, ultra-republican American mining engineer who stumbles on a lost underground civilisation. The Vril-ya, as they are called, enjoy a utopian, perfectly stable social organisation based on 'vril', a source of infinitely renewable electrical power. (Commerce promptly invented the name 'Bovril', the beef essence drink, which, alas, has pleased the public taste rather longer than the novel that inspired it.)

Also present in the Vril-ya's subterranean world are ray guns, aerial travel, ESP and super-advanced technology. The hero falls in love with an alien princess who helps him escape. The novel ends with an ominous prophecy that the superior race will invade the surface of the earth and destroy its earthlings – 'the Darwinian proposition', as Bulwer-Lytton calls it.

Frankenstein, The Battle of Dorking and The Coming Race were the generic stepping stones to H. G. Wells's scientific romances, which – like Holmes – reached their first readers through the cheap end-of-century magazines aimed at those Bovril-sipping masses emancipated into literacy by the 1870 Universal Education Act, with a tanner (sixpence) to spend on weekly magazines. In time, they graduated into pulp paperback form, particularly in America. There has been a similar mutation, in our time, with graphic novels. Bookshops, conservative by instinct, were traditionally reluctant to stock 'comics' (Batman, Superman and all that kids' stuff) – wares beneath their dignity. Leave them to the newsagents. In the face of this resistance, the manufacturers clapped their comics between hard covers. Bookstores promptly accepted them. A new popular genre was born. No Waterstones or Borders now does not have its graphic fiction rack. The genre has its own masters (Neil Gaiman, Frank Miller, etc.) and is growing faster than any other – partly thanks to the ease with which it appeals to the floating constituencies of both comic readers, movie-goers and pulp fiction addicts.

Readerships and bookshops have always played a decisive role in the emergence and mutations of a genre. Readers tend to be genre-loyal ('addicted' might be a better word) – and voracious. It is estimated, for example, that sf fans, who tend to be young, male and college educated, will consume up to a dozen titles a month – burning up the new book shelves.

So, too, with Mills and Boon or Harlequin romances, whose female consumers, surveys reveal, are also often college educated: and why not?

It is the peculiarity of women's popular romance that it likes a high degree of plot repetition between novels – with only small variations. The imprints' websites nowadays have rules to be followed as regards narrative formulae. Nurse Smith finds true love with Doctor Brown, Nurse Brown finds true love with Doctor Smith. My grandmother, who was addicted to 'romances' borrowed, or sometimes nicked, from her twopenny library, would put a cross (her 'mark', poor, semi-literate old woman) on the flyleafs of the novels she had read, to spare herself the waste of reading them again. But since the novels were so similar it scarcely seemed worth wasting the pencil lead.

The voracity of their readers, as has been often observed, encourages over-production by leading genre authors. Western writers Zane Grey (*Riders of the Purple Sage* (1912)), Max Brand (*Destry Rides Again* (1930)) and Louis L'Amour – whose readers tended on the whole not to be college educated – racked up individual title scores in the hundreds. L'Amour had them stacked up so high they kept coming for years after his death. Brand was nicknamed 'the man with the red-hot typewriter'. So were most of the leaders of the genre. Stephen King, in the 'firestorm' phase of his horror-writing career, was turning out three doorstop-sized volumes a year (fuelled, as he later confessed in his semi-autobiography, *On Writing* (2000), by a 16-can case of Budweiser every night).

With the arrival of the internet, genre readerships have found new ways to mobilise themselves – something less clunky than the traditional fanzine. Take, for example, the new age fantasy writer Robert Jordan. When it came out in mid-October 2005 his *Knife of Dreams* shot to the top of the hardback American bestseller list and, the same week, into the UK top ten. Jordan's American publisher, Tor Books, were unsurprised. They had authorised a million-copy first print run.

In the two big Anglophone literary markets, *Knife of Dreams* caters to hardcore initiates. If you have to ask who Robert Jordan is, you will probably never know or care to find out. According to Amazon's 'they also bought this' sheet, those who like *Knife of Dreams* also go for the sword and sorcery and pseudo-religious sagas of George R. R. Martin, Terry Goodkind, Raymond E. Feist, Robin Hobb and Fritz Leiber – names which ring few bells with the general reader. All of them have their genre-loyal fans, mobilised into web-active ganglia, exchanging lore, latest news and interpretative lines on their author. The sites themselves are hieratic – designed for initiates, not outsiders.

Jordan (real name James Oliver Rigney, Jr) is, as it happens, an ex-Vietnam vet who boldly asserts that he will not stop writing until they clamp the coffin lid on his face. His other bestselling line of fiction is a recycling of the Conan the Barbarian epic. On the American version of *Desert Island Discs*, Jordan chose his trusty M16 rifle as one of the three objects he would most like to take with him to his desert island. Like dog-owners and their pets, authors, it seems, come to resemble their heroes.

Knife of Dreams is the eleventh in 'The Wheel of Time' cycle of books following mankind's career from genesis to final showdown. The scale is biblical – and so is the cosmology. At the moment of creation the Creator banishes the 'Dark One', Shai'tan, imprisoning him in a cave outside time and its gigantic wheel. Humans subsequently break into Shai'tan's gaol, breaking its seals and releasing horrors upon their world. The connecting strand of the series follows al'Thor, Rand [sic], a hero who can 'channel' the primal power that drives the wheel. Rand, a child of light, is currently shaping up for his final battle with the Dark One. Initiates, I gather, read all the previous books before embarking on the new one. Those not up to speed will need a glossary and a quick trip to the website.

In book trade terms, 'WoT' (as 'WoTmaniacs' like to call it) is a prime example of 'franchise fiction' – spinning off, profitably, into computer games, comics and sponsored competitions. This latest title has been promoted by an internet hunt, in which experts must navigate twelve riddling websites in order to win their prize. There is a theoryland website (http://www.theoryland.com/theories) devoted to exegesis of the finer points of Jordanology.

The first in the 'WoT' series, *The Eye of the World* came out in 1990. Jordan aims to complete his series in twelve volumes. Both the 'WoT' and the Conan the Barbarian series are currently at the penultimate, Armageddon stage of their grand narratives. The final battle between the forces of light and darkness is coming soon.

It is tempting to read Jordan's fantasia as an allegory of current, real world American anxieties – about creationism, for example. Darwinists, despite their recent court victories, should be apprehensive about the popularity of Jordan's series. George Bush could well be a fan. He is a creationist at heart ('The jury is still out on evolution', he has said – a view with which over half his fellow countrymen concur, apparently). Jordan's vision of a final decisive battle clearly coincides with aspects of the president's world view. Interestingly, sales of Jordan's series jumped after 9/11.

The concluding novel in Jordan's series will come out in 2008, when we will learn the outcome of Rand's final battle against the Dark One. By then we should also know if George Bush has defeated his Dark Ones – or left that task to his luckless successor.

This kind of web mobilisation which propelled *Knife of Dreams* to the number one spot also accounts for the similarly superselling Left Behind cycle (level pegging with Jordan), Tim LaHaye's and Jerry B. Jenkins's fictionalisation of the Book of Revelation (see www.Leftbehind.com). The LaHaye–Jenkins series was, like the planet itself, in its endtime in 2005. The narrative was by now seven years post-rapture (that is, the sudden snatching into heaven of the righteous which constituted the narrative of the dramatic opening volume) and the ensuing tribulation for the 'Left Behind' – those who would have to fight the good fight in order to gain entrance to heaven (or not). Armageddon and the Final Judgement were in prospect. Unlike Harry Potter (also due for its cyclical closure in 2008) the outcome – since the script had already been written by St John – was not in much doubt. However, that was not something to put off Left Behind initiates.

It is sobering (or, if you are evangelically inclined, intoxicating) to learn that the series has sold some thirty million. Surveys suggest that many more millions of Americans believe implicitly that the Final Judgement will come in their lifetime. Following the fall of the Berlin Wall in 1989 and 9/11 the 'religious bestseller' genre has gone from strength to strength in the United States. It fills, presumably, the gaping hole where anti-communism used to be. It defines what it is to be American just as, a hundred years earlier, the then superseliingly popular western propagandised Frederick Jackson Turner's 'frontier thesis' – the notion that only at the frontier, where civilisation meets the wilderness, will the national 'steel' be forged. The contention underlies a whole genre of westerns and cowboy action stories. Who is the 'truer' American, Woody Allen or John Wayne?

My advice on genre fiction is the same as my advice on fiction generally – but writ large. Know yourself (not, I hasten to add, know what you like, which leads to sadly impoverished reading habits). And, if you do not know yourself, look at the genre fiction on your shelves. The reflection there is you. These are group preference novels, and it is important to work out which group you belong to, or want to join. But would I, as Groucho Marx might ask, want to belong to any group that would have me as a reader?

Most readers, if I am anything to go by, move in and out of genre addictions over the course of a reading lifetime. For a decade in my twenties and thirties, it was science fiction (then in a state of genre war between traditional 'hard' sf and 'new wave'). Then crime. I have never really liked old-style, golden age detective fiction on the grounds that I resent any novel that makes me feel stupid. For the same rather shaming reason I find John Le Carré's intricately wrought spy thrillers unpalatable. I could never work out what Smiley or Karla were up to. Thrillers with a comic twist, Elmore Leonard, for example, or others in the Florida subgenre – Dave Barry, Tim Dorsey, Carl Hiaasen – are nowadays increasingly to my taste. So, too, is the London vernacular gangster fiction of Jake Arnott, with its strong flavour of 'Truecrime', as he has trademarked it (for example, in *The Long Firm* (1999) Harry Stark = Reggie Kray; the name is, as puzzle-solving readers have pointed out, an anagram of 'R. Kray Trash').

In no area of fiction is the rule 'by their novels shall ye know them', truer than it is in genre. The only advice I can usefully give is: experiment from time to time. Who knows, old man, there may be *something* in the teen fiction racks; after all, Philip Pullman is there.

chapter 16

Getting physical

CONTEMPLATING THE NOVEL is one thing: picking it up – 'getting into it', as we say – is quite another. It is instructive, again, to watch fellow browsers in the bookstore. They love to handle the wares. They don't just 'finger' the book, they 'thumb' it. It is no accident that we call a much-read volume 'well-thumbed'. Using the opposable thumb is, for our species, immensely satisfying. This is one reason that among the young 'texting' (which requires virtuosic use of the thumb) and computer games (which, typically, are also thumb-operated) are so addictive.

Books, also, need the thumb for efficient reading. Homo sapiens is also Homo pollex. But more than just the thumb is involved in our physical engagement with the book. The physical act of reading will typically involve snapping the volume open (the sound of the spine cracking is an added thrill), licking the index finger to turn the page, angling the book this way and that, turning down the page to mark one's place. Unfortunately, the uncut novel is a thing of the past except in ultra-civilised France. There are few reading pleasures equal to slitting pages as you read, with the kind of stiletto with which you could, at a pinch, hold up a convenience store.

One of the few things I resent about the public library culture I grew up with is the fencing off of the margin – writing in the margin was a 'mutilation' of public property and seriously criminal, as the luckless Joe Orton and Kenneth Halliwell discovered when they 'improved' Islington public library books with their mischievous decorations (now expensive *objets d'art*). Paper is expensive and used to be more so (though less expensive, granted, than lamb bellies). But from the first printed books onwards, generous white margins were left as they had been in the codex's manuscript predecessor. It would have been easy for compositors, then and now, to print flush against all four page edges. Instead, some 10 per cent of the page surface is left temptingly white. For what? Marginalia, of course. Commentary. *Nota benes*. The four-sided, flush, verso–recto-balanced margin, standard in every novel, is a hangover from the age of manuscript, when they were there for the 'commentator' – a contributor who would add in marginalia, running heads, footnotes, corrections, embellishments. Now they are great white empty spaces – the result of cultural inertia.

No one at this late and commercially standardised stage of the publishing industry is going to redesign the architecture of the traditional book. It will stay as it is until it is superseded by something technologically more advanced. But all that virgin white space cries out to be used. Personally, I find it satisfying to read even fiction pencil in hand. A pen is going too far, and if you are leaning back you often cannot get ballpoints to write: the ink sort of dries up – why does not some inventor do something about that?

Whether you use it or not, the pencil-in-hand elevates you to the status of player, rather than mere consumer. It renders you, in the term beloved by computerists, interactive. And frequently enough when reading fiction I itch to use the pencil. Take the following – a passage which I think is one of the most sublime written in late twentieth-century fiction. It is the widening horizon fade-out at the conclusion of Salman Rushdie's *Midnight's Children* (1981):

> Yes, they will trample me underfoot, the numbers marching one two three, four hundred million five hundred six, reducing me to specks of voiceless dust, just as, in all good time, they will trample my son who is not my son, and his son who will not be his, and his who will not be his, and his who will not be his, until the thousand and first generation, until a thousand and one midnights have bestowed their terrible gifts and a thousand and one children have died, because it is the privilege and the curse of midnight's children to be both masters and victims of their times, to forsake privacy and be sucked into the annihilating whirlpool of the multitudes, and to be unable to live or die in peace.

Alongside the margin, in my copy, where the novelist writes about 600 million, I have added the note, 'now a billion plus!!'

It is a feeble riposte that the novelist, of course, can never hear. But it puts the reader, so to speak, inside the novel.

E-novels have been available, free of charge, on the internet for over a decade. Why, then, is it that otherwise computer-proficient readers shell out up to a tenner for a reprint classic edition of *Bleak House* (serialised, for a viewing audience of six

Mughal Emperor I shall die with Kashmir on my lips, unable to see the valley of delights to which men go to enjoy life, or to end it, or both; because now I see other figures in the crowd, the terrifying figure of a war-hero with lethal knees, who has found out how I cheated him of his birthright, he is pushing towards me through the crowd which is now wholly composed of familiar faces, there is Rashid the rickshaw boy arm-in-arm with the Rani of Cooch Naheen, and Ayooba Shaheed Farooq with Mutasim the Handsome, and from another direction, the direction of Haji Ali's island tomb, I see a mythological apparition approaching, the Black Angel, except that as it nears me its face is green its eyes are black, a center-parting in its hair, on the left green and on the right black, its eyes the eyes of Widows; Shiva and the Angel are closing closing, I hear lies being spoken in the night, anything you want to be you kin be, the greatest lie of all, cracking now, fission of Saleem, I am the bomb in Bombay, watch me explode, bones splitting breaking beneath the awful pressure of the crowd, bag of bones falling down down down, just as once at Jallianwala, but Dyer seems not to be present today, no Mercurochrome, only a broken creature spilling pieces of itself into the street, because I have been so-many too-many persons, life unlike syntax allows one more than three, and at last somewhere the striking of a clock, twelve chimes, release.

Yes, they will trample me underfoot, the numbers marching one two three, four hundred million five hundred six, reducing me to specks of voiceless dust, just as, in all good time, they will trample my son who is not my son, and his son who will not be his, and his who will not be his, until the thousand and first generation, until a thousand and one midnights have bestowed their terrible gifts and a thousand and one children have died, because it is the privilege and the curse of midnight's children to be both masters and victims of their times, to forsake privacy and be sucked into the annihilating whirlpool of the multitudes, and to be unable to live or die in peace.

now a billion plus!!

Guerrilla annotation

million-plus on the BBC in late 2005) rather than reading it, for nothing, on www.gutenberg.com?

Ancient as it is, as asserted in Chapter 3, the paper-and-ink codex remains a more efficient container of narrative than the e-text, which is, essentially, an electronic scroll with all the shortcomings of its papyrus ancestor. Alan Turing, father of the modern computer, perceived the book's superiority over digitised text in that the book can be cut into anywhere. You can carry out operations (via the index, chapter-and-verse, or pagination reference) which computers find laborious; and computer users even more so. Gripping novels are often called page-turners, but often the reader wants to go backwards as well as forwards, to skip around the narrative: either to check out some detail, or simply to relish something again. Easily done with a book. Less easily done with an iMac and its search function.

Ideally, the novel should be a whole body experience. Reading can use legs (to fetch the book down from the bookshelf, for example), arms (reaching up for it), hands (holding it), fingers and thumbs (flicking the pages), mouth (licking the finger). It can be done at the table, on the sofa, in the train, on the plane. Interestingly, among the young it seems to becoming an even more physical activity. The austerely academic historian of reading Armando Petrucci reports (rather anxiously) in *A History of Reading in the West* (1999):

> How can we describe the new *modus legendi* of young readers? First of all, the body takes totally free positions determined by individual preferences: a reader can stretch out on the floor, lean against a wall, sit under (yes under) a reading room table, sit with his or her feet up on a table

(the oldest and most widespread stereotype) and so on
... the new *modus legendi* also includes a physical relationship with the book that is more intense and direct than
in traditional modes of reading. The book is constantly
manipulated, crumpled, bent, forced in various direc-
tions and carried on the body. One might say that readers
make it their own by an intensive, prolonged and violent
use more typical of a relationship of consumption than of
reading and learning.

Librarians, for whom all patrons are potential Ortons and
Halliwells, might disagree. But greater physicality with the
book is a fact of modern reading. Obscurely, I feel, it goes
together with the greater independence, confidence and self-
assertiveness of modern (particularly young) readers.

chapter 17

See as well as read

ARE THE FOLLOWING the same opening sentence?

It was the best of times, it was the worst of times, it was
the age of wisdom, it was the age of foolishness, it was
the epoch of belief, it was the epoch of incredulity, it was
the season of Light, it was the season of Darkness, it was
the spring of hope, it was the winter of despair, we had
everything before us, we had nothing before us, we were
all going direct to Heaven, we were all going direct the
other way – in short, the period was so far like the present
period, that some of its noisiest authorities insisted on
its being received, for good or for evil, in the superlative
degree of comparison only.

It was the best of times, it was the worst of times, it was the
age of wisdom, it was the age of foolishness, it was the epoch
of belief, it was the epoch of incredulity, it was the season
of Light, it was the season of Darkness, it was the spring of
hope, it was the winter of despair, we had everything before

us, we had nothing before us, we were all going direct to Heaven, we were all going direct the other way – in short, the period was so far like the present period, that some of its noisiest authorities insisted on its being received, for good or for evil, in the superlative degree of comparison only.

It was the best of times, it was the worst of times, it was the age of wisdom, it was the age of foolishness, it was the epoch of belief, it was the epoch of incredulity, it was the season of Light, it was the season of Darkness, it was the spring of hope, it was the winter of despair, we had everything before us, we had nothing before us, we were all going direct to Heaven, we were all going direct the other way – in short, the period was so far like the present period, that some of its noisiest authorities insisted on its being received, for good or for evil, in the superlative degree of comparison only.

These three versions of the opening sentence of A Tale of Two Cities (1859) are, of course, word by word the same text. Materially they are chalk and cheese; as different as the same words uttered by different mouths. The degree to which we see what is on the page, as opposed to merely read it – see through it, as it were, is debatable. Arguably the job of the novel, done well, is to 'transport' us, carry us away. Those tiny black marks on an only slightly larger white surface are a portal – a kind of stargate into another world.

On the other hand, from the first to the last word in a novel, it is only a typographic link which keeps us online. Once the type stops, the novel stops. American hardback designers typically give careful (sometimes extravagant) thought to the best kind of font to be used, of the thousands available. Often there will be a little-read colophon explaining this, like the following from the last printed page of Truman Capote's 'lost' novel, *Summer Crossing* (rediscovered in 2005, suspiciously coincidentally with the release of a big budget biopic of the author):

> About the Type
> This book is set in Fournier, a typeface named for Pierre Simon Fournier, the youngest son of a French printing family. He started out engraving woodblocks and large capitals, then moved on to fonts of type. In 1736 he began his own foundry and made several important contributions in the field of type design; he is said to have cut 147 alphabets of his own creation. Fournier is probably best remembered as the designer of St Augustine Ordinaire, a face that served as the model of Monotype's Fournier, which was released in 1925.

It is an impressive lecturette on printing history. But in what sense does it enhance a novel, about a predecessor of Holly Golightly? (Think Audrey Hepburn – and would the character have been different had she been played by Shirley MacLaine?) She is described in the blurb to *Summer Crossing* as: 'Grady – beautiful, rich, flame-haired, defiant – is the sort of girl people stare at across a room.' Would Capote's novel have suffered any detraction had it been set in Times New Roman, Bembo or Lucida Sans Unicode, or tattooed on human skin?

My sense is that the physical forms of a novel, unless it is a de luxe, author-signed edition, will not matter much to many readers who are neither bibliophiles nor students of book history. Most readers may not even register, after putting down the book, what the type looked like, so long as it was untroubling to the eye. Similarly, few readers are worried by the sometimes drastic hyphenation which the flush right

Chapter 1

"You are a mystery, my dear," her mother said, and Grady, gazing across the table through a centerpiece of roses and fern, smiled indulgently: yes, I am a mystery, and it pleased her to think so. But Apple, eight years older, married, far from mysterious, said: "Grady is only foolish; I wish I were going with you. Imagine, Mama, this time next week you'll be having breakfast in Paris! George ke͏͏ ͏ ͏mising that we'll go . . . I don't know, though." Sh͏ ͏ ͏ ͏ ͏ ͏ ͏ ͏ ͏ ͏ed at her sister. "Grady, why on earth ͏ ͏ ͏ New York in the dead of summe͏ ͏ ͏ ͏ ͏ ͏ ͏ ͏ ͏ ͏ would leave her alone; still this ͏ ͏ ͏ the very morning the boat saile͏ ͏ ͏ ͏ ͏ ͏ ͏e-yond what she'd said? After ͏ ͏ ͏ ͏ ͏th, and the truth she did not e͏ ͏ ͏ ͏ ͏ ͏ ͏ ͏never (justified) margins enforce. For some reason ragged right (unjustified) looks wrong to the novel-reader's eye.

None the less expertise in this area is growing, due largely to the font libraries and layout variations nowadays made available by Microsoft word processing programmes. In general novels – particularly 'gripping' novels which encourage fast or breakneck reading – benefit from large point size (this book is set in 10pt) and generous 'leading' (the gap between the lines). The American edition of *Summer Crossing*, for example, looks to me like 11 on 13 point. Non-fiction books concerned with packaging, or packing in, information will be much more solid.

A gappy page was normal in the nineteenth century when readers were generally less proficient than they are now, and many needed type not much smaller than a toddler's alphabet blocks in order to read at all. Additionally, novelists were encouraged to have lots of short-line dialogue so that the print had white space through which to run its three-volume length.

Today new novels, although usually packed looser than non-fiction, are markedly tighter on the page than their nineteenth-century predecessors. The budget packaging of the paperback reprint encourages a 'solid' page, and a more constipated reading. Point size is a small thing – a 72nd of an inch, to be precise. But be alert to it. Consciously, or unconsciously, it may affect your reading comfort. From time to time break away to *look* at the page, not just *read* it.

chapter 18

Hardback or paperback?

TRY THE FOLLOWING TEST. Confronted in a bookshop (walk-in or electronic) by a glossy new paperback of, say, Michael Connelly's 2005/6 bestseller *The Lincoln Lawyer* and – in the bargain section – a remaindered hardback of the same novel at exactly the same price, which of the books would you choose and what factors would be operating in your making that choice?

My guess is that the average novel reader would weigh up the convenience of portability (the paperback is, in origin, a 'pocket book'; the hardback a 'library book') against the convenience of legibility and durability. The hardback is tougher and its print larger and more contrastive against good quality paper, easier on the eye. This calculation, I suspect, is going on, one way or another, everywhere around you in a large bookshop. But, of course, the two versions are, normally, not available at the same time. Paperbacks usually come out many months later than the hardback – that delay is the penalty paid by the eager reader for the reduced pain in his wallet. So the other determining factor, when confronted with a desirable hardback, is: 'Am I prepared to wait for the paperback – given that it may be a year or so coming?'

'You pay nothing for my book, sir,' went the early nineteenth-century advertisement, 'you only pay for the binding.' So it is today. If you buy the new hardback it will cost three times as much as the later paperback reprint. And, of course, you are paying for features that – given the short shelf life of most novels – you may not want.

The emergence of the publisher-bound novel is intimately connected with the growth of the great circulating libraries in the mid nineteenth century. The hardbacked (often ornately bound) three-volume novel cost, from the 1830s until the 1890s, an outrageous guinea and a half – equivalent to about £80 in current value. No one other than the libraries (and not even them the full amount) paid thirty-one shillings and sixpence for *Jane Eyre* in February 1847. There was, the Victorian joke went, one reader who had bought a new three-decker, but no one could remember his name.

Avid readers of 'Currer Bell's' new novel ('is the hussy Thackeray's mistress, as the *Quarterly Review* alleges? and him, the rascal with a mad wife in his attic') borrowed the mouth-watering thing, a volume at a time, from Mudie's library – whose subscriptions started at a mere guinea a year per volume. Mr Mudie, although he did not, Scottish presbyterian that he was, approve of 'fast' fiction, was no fool: the single three-decker novel could keep three customers happy at the same time.[24]

Public libraries in the mid twentieth century reckoned that a hardback novel was good for 150 loans before falling apart, or before its pages rotted from all the licked fingers turning them (there were, inevitably, grim suspicions that library books carried TB, or worse). The motive for hard-backing your fiction had changed with the industrialisation of the book world. When Mr Bennet of Longbourn, or Squire Shandy up there in Yorkshire had their books calf-bound, bookplated and gilt-tooled, it was to make them handsome for their private shelves and to preserve them for posterity. Not to make them accessible to innumerable hands and the bespittled fingers of strangers. As well put their daughters on the streets (although Lydia Bennet would have taken to the trade better than most Austen heroines).

There have, from the 1830s onwards, always been cheap reprints of fiction, costing from a fifth to a third of the initial price, usually appearing at an interval of six months to two years after first publication – so that the expensive form can have its run. Allen Lane took this one stage further with his first Penguins in 1935, but it was the 'paperback revolution' of the 1960s which effectively set up the two-tier system we now have.

Why, then, when novels in the first decade of the twentieth-first century are predominantly bought, not borrowed, are new novels issued in the anachronistic 'library' edition at standard prices of around £17 or $25? Why does the booktrade perpet-uate this anomaly? There are a number of reasons:

1. The hardback is, like the aircraft carrier, a superb, if somewhat over-engineered, platform. It can support a dustjacket which fairly buzzes with information, artwork and publicity material. It can also, given its price, warrant good paper and type. All of which, like a luxury saloon car, attracts the discerning reader. There is no reason why we should not all be driving around in shoe-boxed size Smart cars, or fifteen-year-old (but still with lots of go in them) Skodas. But, demonstrably, many car owners prefer something classier.

2. The hardback generates money which supports an ambitious publishing programme, allowing a wide diversity of novels, handsomely produced – only a few of which will make money – to be produced. It acts as a kind of trial balloon. Fewer than half (it used to be a fifth) of hardbacks make it to paperback. Given the high profitability on a low volume of sale, the hardback keeps the aperture for the production of fiction wide open.

3. Hardbacks get reviewed. Paperbacks, at best, get noticed. Most, alas, come and go beneath notice.

4. Hardbacks are durable. Paperbacks are consumable. Hardbacks give cultural stability to one's life.

Many consumers of fiction exercise a kind of triage over reading choices. Will I dig into my pocket now or 'wait for the paperback'? Impulse purchase or strategic waiting game? There is, demonstrably, high price resistance – of a purely psychological kind – which operates in bookshops. 'Why should I buy the new Nick Hornby, A Long Way Down, for seventeen quid, when I can get High Fidelity, which I haven't read yet (though I saw the movie), for £6.99?'

The resistance is heightened by the fact that, in most cases, a novel is read only once, straight through, and never again. Non-fiction books are more likely to be revisited and less likely to be tossed aside. If, at Christmas 2005, you bought Danielle Steel's Toxic Bachelors and Schott's Miscellany (both riding high on their respective bestseller lists), which would be more likely to be on the coffee table, for casual dipping into, during the long evenings of June 2006? (Or, perhaps, which would you rather have seen on your coffee table?)

But the fact is, hardback novels (particularly after 1995 in the UK, when retail price maintenance was abolished and bookshops started discounting) are cheaper in real terms than ever before in book history, and represent superb value. They are also more glamorous – erotic even. A former colleague of mine, Steve Quartz (a cognitive biologist), has been recruited by Hollywood, the Los Angeles Times informs me, to do neuro-marketing on films – to get into the brains of the audience (think Malcolm McDowell in A Clockwork Orange) to ascertain what endings, for example, 'work'.

Were the same exercise undertaken for books, I suspect Professor Quartz would discover that buying a hardback gives a distinct sexual thrill. The paperback, by contrast, probably gives no more than a warm glow around the wallet. Neuro-market research will doubtless confirm this proposition quite soon.

As etymology suggests, there is an intimate link between novelty – newness – and the novel. Even if bought at a full price, the novel, furnishing as it does an average of five hours' pleasure, is a cheaper date than the movies, theatre, opera or World Federation Wrestling. Multi-channel subscription television is cheaper, but most of it, despite all the pseudo choice, is not worth watching and in many cases you still have the intolerable intrusion of advertisements for non-book commodities – something that, mercifully, novels have not succumbed to. (Dickens's serials, of course, were encased in their monthly form in an 'advertiser', touting everything from ladies' corsets to gentlemen's hair restorer but the practice has not, despite the ingenuity of the industry, survived).

Hardback, dustjacketed novels which are, particularly in America, things of physical beauty, furnish a thrill of acqui-sition and ownership which the bargain-price reprint, with its glue binding, low-quality paper and frequently tacky cover does not. The advice is: always go for the hardback if you really want to read a novel. Apart from anything else, the deterrently high price will make you think carefully about whether you really want to read the thing. Which is good. And, observably, one reads a hardback more respectfully. Reserve the paperback for titles which, for one reason or another, you have missed.

Price

If, unWoolfianly, you follow the above advice and routinely buy hardback the chances are you will not have to pay full whack (the publisher's rrp, or recommended retail price). It was possible, for example, using Ted Smart's Book People mail-or-web order service to buy the whole 2005 Man Booker shortlist – all six titles – for a mere £29.99 (plus £2.50 for speedy delivery to your door), saving some £90 on the rrp and the back-breaking labour of lugging the things home. Such bargains are increasingly available to the moderately canny novel buyer.

Hardbacks will be discounted in retail outlets for three reasons, which it is worth bearing in mind when making the Solomonic choice of which new novel to choose of the hundreds on offer?:

1. The retailer regards them as loss leaders, sprats to catch mackerel. Once you have put the discounted book in your basket you will buy others; or so the retailer hopes. This may predispose you to buy and leave, like a poker player who leaves the table while he is ahead. Few do, apparently.

2. The novel is selling so well that economy of scale has kicked in, and profits can be made on a substantially

lower cover price. This may make you think twice. Why come in at the tail of the reading pack?

3. The novel has been over-ordered. Rather than go through the tedious business of sale and return, the bookseller is dumping stock. Other readers *don't* want it.

It pays to work out which, or which combination, of these factors is in play before you reach for your wallet.

chapter 19

What do you do with the novel? Read it, listen to it, look at it?

ONE MAY AS well begin (to echo Zadie Smith echoing E.M. Forster) with the beginning of Salman Rushdie's 2005 novel, *Shalimar the Clown*:

> At twenty-four the ambassador's daughter slept badly through the warm, unsurprising nights. She woke up frequently and even when sleep did come her body was rarely at rest, thrashing and flailing as if trying to break free of dreadful invisible manacles. At times she cried out in a language she did not speak ... According to one report she sounded guttural, glottal-stoppy, as if she were speaking Arabic. Night-Arabian, she thought, the dream-tongue of Scheherazade. Another version described her words as science-fictional, like Klingon.

This is Salman at his most flamboyantly Salmanic. But the rhapsodic overture embodies a fundamental truth about the art of fiction. Like Scheherazade, the teller of the Arabian

Nights' 1001 tales, who will die should her tales ever cease or cease to amuse her audience of one, latterday fictioneers must create their particular dreamtongue. Every original work of fiction patents its own language. Its idiolect – a way of speaking which is as readily discernible as mine is from yours and everybody else's.

On the other hand, Scheherazade's head would soon lie steaming in the executioner's basket should she resolve to go all the idiolectical way and regale her captious, story-loving lord in Klingon. Fiction is all about compromise: finding the precarious balance between self-expression and serving the reader.

There is a revealing moment in Monica Ali's 2003 saga of first-generation immigrant life in East London, Brick Lane, when the heroine, Nazneen, hears a new word: 'Hospital, hospital, hospital. She had another English word. She caressed it all the way down the corridor.'

A Londoner who does not know the word 'hospital'? What is this? I suspect other Anglophone readers were, like me, pulled up short by the sudden realisation that the novel is happening (linguistically) not in the Queen's English, but in Bangla.

If Brick Lane were stylistically ethical it would have been written throughout in a dialect which would have restricted its circulation to Brick Lane itself, not the millions in the English speaking world who bought it. The novelist who wants to get on to the bestseller lists and into the educational curricula (as Ali, happily, has done) must reach out; and, where required, sell out.

Walter Scott got to grips with the problem in his early nineteenth-century historical novels. How, in Ivanhoe, written in 1819 and set in the fourteenth century, could one have an authentic-seeming style of dialogue and description that

would neither weary the reader with dry-as-dust antiquari-
anism nor render itself absurd with theatrical 'tushery' and
'gadzookery'? A slight stiltedness was Scott's solution; as in,
for example: '"By my halidome," said Fitzurse, "the plan was
worthy of your united wisdom."' It sounds slightly different,
but is not entirely offputting – even to modern readers who
do not know their halidome from the Millennium Dome. No
contemporary of Richard the Lionheart actually spoke that
way. But the 'slight stiltedness' device enables the reader to
get into *Ivanhoe*'s long distant past.

An impressive, and deservedly much praised historical
novel published in 2005 is James Meek's *The People's Act of
Love*. It is written by a British writer for an English-speaking
public. The action is set in Siberia in 1919 around a historically unregarded sideshow of the Revolution, the part played
by the Czech Legion.

The idiom of the novel, as confected by Meek, is cunningly
off-key. At one point, for example, a member of a sect of
fanatic Siberian self-mutilates announces: 'I am castrated.
And I am happy.' I cannot imagine any eunuch brought up in
the English tongue saying it quite like that. Meek contrives,
though, with his carefully measured stiltedness, to avoid the
woodenness of standard translations from the Russian. But
there remain moments when, for all the stylistic poise, the
narrative wobbles. In the following, for example:

> Viktor Timofeyevich Skachkov, Land Captain of Yazyk,
> was eating breakfast alone in the dining room when his
> wife shrieked the name of God three times upstairs, each
> time louder than the last, then let out a long howl, which
> rolled from high to low, ending in a gurgle of pure found-
> edness, like a baby laughing.

What, precisely, is a 'Land Captain'? To the Anglophone ear it sounds like Toyota's latest SUV. How is shrieking 'the name of God' different from shrieking 'God'? What, in that God's name, is 'a gurgle of pure foundedness'?

Overdo the stilted bits and the novel topples. This, alas, happens in Uzodinma Iweala's *Beasts of No Nation*, an 'I-narrated' account of a boy soldier's experiences in Africa's never-ending civil wars which rather flopped in the UK in 2005, but received a chorus of rave reviews in the US in 2006. Among other overwhelming scenes of horror is the lad being raped in the line of duty by his 'commandant':

> Then he is saying, remove your clothe [sic]. So I was removing them. And then, after making me be touching his soldier and all of that thing with my hand and with my tongue and lip he was telling me to kneel and then he was entering inside of me the way the man goat is sometimes mistaking other man goat for woman goat and going inside of them.

The bestial goat has neither nation nor language. Nor does this infantile warrior. Iweala (a writer with roots in Nigeria and a degree in creative writing from Harvard) bequeaths his hero a primitive pidgin. One can see, and even respect, why it is done. But it grates alienatingly on the ear.

Just as works of fiction (the best of them, at least) craft their own idiolect, so do they carry unique authorial markers. So distinctive are they that a literary cryptanalyst like Professor Don Foster (the FBI's most called-on academic) can – as he did with Joe Klein, 'Anonymous' and *Primary Colors* – identify authorship as authoritatively as the forensic scientist identifies a criminal by voice print. The task is rarely so difficult that we need to call upon the professor. If he saw lines of *The Prelude* running wild in the deserts of Arabia, Coleridge said, he would shout 'Wordsworth!' Who, reading *Shalimar*'s opening paragraph, wandering wild in Los Angeles or – if you were suicidally inclined – Arabia, would not shout 'Rushdie!'?

It takes a long time, the trumpeter Miles Davis said, before you can play like yourself; or write like Rushdie. It can also, on the reader's part, take a long time to learn not merely how to read, but how to *hear* a novel. *Finnegans Wake* (1939), James Joyce asserted, requires a lifetime's listening. The boilerplate prose of Jeffrey Archer and his invisible editorial collaborators can be mastered in the two-hour delay between check-in and take-off.

'Read, read, and read the Victorians,' the historian G. M. Young liked to instruct his students, 'until you can *hear* them.' It is not just a matter of grinding away. Tuning one's set so as to hear a novel is tricky. Rushdie, as his public readings make clear, likes his prose to go at a rattling pace – allegro. J. M. Coetzee, as the title of his 2005 novel, *Slow Man*, signals and its opening lines confirm, is adagio:

> The blow catches him from the right, sharp and surprising and painful, like a bolt of electricity, lifting him up off the bicycle. *Relax!* he tells himself as he flies through the air (*flies through the air with the greatest of ease!*), and indeed he can feel his limbs go obediently slack. *Like a cat* he tells himself: roll, *then spring to your feet, ready for what comes next.* The unusual word *limber* or *limbre* is on the horizon too.

The words drop like single pebbles into a deep well. The intervals sometimes seem longer than the words themselves.

And should the mind's ear insert a vowel-flattened South African ('Sith Ifricin') accent? The hero, Paul Rayment, is French by origin. Should that condiment ('limbre') also go into the auditory mix? The action is set in Adelaide – perhaps, then, a dash of "Strine'?

John Banville's meditative and retrospective *The Sea* insists on being heard as a langorous internal monologue, with an Irish inflection and an old man's weariness of manner. The novel swells gently, like the element of the title – a feature which some reviewers have found tedious. Again the opening lines will serve:

> They departed, the gods, on the day of the strange tide. All morning under a milky sky the waters in the bay had swelled and swelled, rising to unheard-of heights, the small waves creeping over parched sand that for years had known no wetting save for rain and lapping the very bases of the dunes.

Caryl Phillips sets himself a complex problem in *Dancing in the Dark*, his 2005 biofiction of the early twentieth-century Afro-American vaudevillian Bert Williams. Off stage a cultivated and melancholy man Williams is required, by the crass prejudices of his white audiences, to play on stage the jolly dancing darkie. His partner George protests eloquently at the racial and linguistic travesty:

> Listen to me, Bert, the so-called character that you're playing is a damn-fool creature who has been created by the white man, and this 'smoke' fixes us now in their minds as hopeless failures. But times have changed now and we should no longer be standing up in front of the white man and delivering simplistic stories with the

right amount of darky naïveté. I mean, let me ask you, how many of our own people are truly happy to eat just watermelon, or fall over on their faces, or mispronounce the English language?

How should George's dignified outrage be 'heard'? Cultivated American? Or cultivated American with a tang ('daamn-fool') of soft black drawl?

Caryl Phillips is not, by linguistic origin, American but Afro-Caribbean. How accurately does he catch the nuances of American speech? Can an outsider ever completely master a tongue, or dialect, in which they were not brought up? Conrad never did, nor did Nabokov, although their failures are magnificent.

Zadie Smith's *On Beauty* is set, virtually entirely, in New England. She herself spent a couple of years there, at Harvard, after the success of *White Teeth*. What accent should the reader's ear impose on the following description of bulimic January in a New England women's hall of residence? Smith's Cambridge, England voice or her Cambridge, Mass. voice?

In January, at the first formal of the year, the tremendous will-power of Wellington's female students is revealed. Unfortunately for the young women, this demonstration of pure will is accredited to 'femininity' – that most passive of virtues – and, as a result, does not contribute to their Grade Point Average. It is unfair. Why are there no awards for a girl who starves herself through the Christmas period?

Snooty cis-Atlantic, homely trans-Atlantic or bland mid-Atlantic? The passage *means* something different in each case.

The acoustics of fiction matter. Our obsessive concern with 'reading' and 'literacy skills' has created a public which has – if not a universal tin ear – a disabling hearing problem when it comes to fiction. Educators could usefully address this issue. So, I think, could the creators and producers of novels, locked as they are in an obstinately soundless print format which has barely changed since Caxton. A hi-tech civilisation which can come up with Christmas cards that sing carols for their recipients can surely invent an electronic tuning fork for fiction. Why not a novel which, when opened, recites for its reader the first paragraph in the author-approved voice?

chapter 20

Real world, fictional world – same world?

BRET EASTON ELLIS'S *Lunar Park* rode very high on the 2005–6 American and UK fiction bestseller lists. Ellis's novel is named after the place where the main action happens. There is – I have checked – no town of that name in New York State, any more than there is a Stepford in Connecticut or an Ambridge in Borsetshire. The hero narrator of *Lunar Park* is 'Bret Easton Ellis'. A real person of that name wrote the novel set in the fictional place. I know he is real – I shook his hand when he came to the UK in October 2005 to promote the British release of his novel.

In a long authorial preface to *Lunar Park*, Bret (let us call him 'Bret') confesses to a life of gargantuan excess after the runaway success of his precociously early supersellers, *Less than Zero* and *American Psycho*, had shot him into bestsell-erdom, millionairedom and the ranks of front-page (*National Enquirer*, that is) celebrity. The young 'Bret' embarked on a bender of conspicuous consumption, fashion trashing and self-indulgence worthy of one of the more disreputable Roman emperors:

I was doing Ray-Ban ads at twenty-two. I was posing for the covers of English magazines on the tennis court, on a throne, on the deck of my condo in a purple robe. I threw lavish parties – sometimes complete with strippers – in my condo on a whim ('Because it's Thursday!' one invitation read). I crashed a borrowed Ferrari in South-ampton and its owner just smiled (for some reason I was naked). I attended three fairly exclusive orgies ... I dined at the White House in the summer of 1986, the guest of Jeb and George W. Bush, both of whom were fans.

The Bushes are real (too real for some of us). I doubt they were ever fans of *Less than Zero*, published in 1985 – even in the hot days of their youth when, as the scandalmongers persistently allege, George did naughty things. And if the Bush boys *were* fans of Ellis's 'black candy', it would be wise to keep it secret now from the religious right which has voted one brother into presidency and the other into state governorship. Cruel of 'Bret' to out them.

Briefly for 'Bret' it was 'top of the world, ma!' But, inevi-tably, under the glare and temptations of celebrity, the young fellow took to heroin, cocaine and vile sexual practices. He ended up lying in a squalid hotel bedroom for seven days 'watching porn DVDs with the sound off and snorting maybe forty bags of heroin, a blue plastic bucket that I vomited in continually by my bed'.

His drive to the blue bucket was, 'Bret' divulges in his preface, fuelled by the death in August 1992 of his father, Robert Martin Ellis, a couple of months after the publication of *American Psycho*. The portrait of Mr Ellis Sr offered in *Lunar Park* is one that most sons would keep in the attic. He was a real-estate crook and 'careless, abusive, alcoholic, vain, angry, paranoid'. Chapter and verse are supplied on these paternal shortcomings.

Bret's dad was, apparently, the original inspiration for Patrick Bateman, the sociopath hero of *American Psycho*. Mr Ellis Sr's dead body, the novel relates, 'was found naked by the twenty-two year old girlfriend on the bathroom floor of his empty house in Newport Beach.' He left, among many squandered millions, a wardrobe of over-sized Armani suits. When 'Bret', who, like Bateman, is partial to Armani, took the clothes to the tailor to be altered:

> I was revolted to discover that most of the inseams in the crotch were stained with blood, which we later found out was the result of a botched penile implant he underwent in Minneapolis.

Robert Martin Ellis was real. He was, I believe, a realtor. He did indeed die in August 1992. *Lunar Park* is dedicated to his memory. Whether it was with a surgically enhanced penis that he went to the crematorium fire, or the unsullied member with which he engendered young Bret, is unrecorded. Literary history may never know.

'Bret Easton Ellis' suspects his love child, Robby, by Jayne Dennis, the woman who later became his wife, was engendered by Keanu Reeves, 'who had been a friend of mine when he was initially cast in *Less than Zero*, [before being] replaced by Andrew McCarthy'. So suspicious was 'Bret' of the actor that he launched a paternity case in which his lawyer asserted in court that Dennis's child 'bears a striking resemblance to a certain Mr Keanu Reeves'. Litigation was subsequently dropped, 'Bret' and Dennis were reconciled, married and went to live in Lunar Park with Robby and a daughter born in wedlock.

Mr Reeves is, so to speak, 'real'. He enjoys, I gather, friendly relations with Mr Ellis. Before becoming a superstar in the *Matrix* trilogy, Reeves was, initially, cast as the lead in the 1987 film of *Less than Zero* and replaced by the equally real Mr McCarthy. Jayne Dennis, although she has a website, is not real. Nor is the dubiously sired Robby Ellis. They are figments of the fictional Lunar Park. Mr Ellis is not married. He has no child. In August 2005 Mr Ellis told *The New York Times* that he was bisexual and that his best friend and lover for six years, Michael Wade Kaplan, had died in January, aged thirty. That is not the history of 'Bret' in *Lunar Park*.

The main narrative of *Lunar Park* chronicles the disintegration of the Ellis–Dennis marriage. Patrick Bateman, the murderous, paternally inspired serial killer of *American Psycho* comes to life off the page and haunts his creator. Mr Bateman is not real. His author is. The author's father was. But perhaps not in Lunar Park.

The comedian Rik Mayall's memoir, immodestly entitled *Bigger than Hitler, Better than Christ*, rode high in the late 2005 non-fiction bestseller list, adjoining the fiction list adorned with *Lunar Park*. But are they all that different in approach? The blurb of Mr Mayall's 'electrifying autobiography' offers a cv strangely reminiscent of 'Bret' reminiscing about his shenanigans with the two sprigs of the Bush dynasty at the White House:

> Rik Mayall invented alternative comedy with *The Young Ones*, he brought down the Thatcher administration with *The New Statesman* and he changed the global culture with his masterpiece *Bottom*. Not only was his number one single 'Living Doll' the saviour of rock 'n roll but he also rescued the British film industry with the vast revenues

created by his legendary movie *Drop Dead Fred*. In 1998, he survived an assassination attempt and spent five days in a coma before he literally came back from the dead.

It is not recorded whether he had a blue bucket by his bed. Rik Mayall did, of course, make his name as 'Rick' in the television comedy series *The Young Ones*. Cliff Richard might disagree about it being Rik's version of 'Living Doll' that made rock history. Fans might disagree that either Cliff or 'Rik' did much for their music.

Recounting episodes from his early career, 'Rik' confides a relationship with a Tony and Mrs Blair:

> I will never openly discuss the love that Cherie and I have made because of the damage that it will do not only to Tony and Cherie themselves but also to the British people. It's not as though I'm going to reveal in print that Cherie and I have been on/off lovers for a long time now, or passionate pillow-biting adulterees as I like to think of us. And, believe me, she can bite a lot of pillow with a mouth like that.

Cherie Blair is real. She has a generously sized mouth. She did not have it off with 'Rik', any more than the Bush brothers snorted coke in the George Washington bedroom with 'Bret'.

In the above accounts I have borrowed W. G. Sebald's convention in his 1998 novel (or is it?) *The Rings of Saturn*, in which he distinguishes, by use of inverted commas, between Max Sebald the author and 'W. G. Sebald' the narrator-wanderer, ruminating about life as he ambles round East Anglia. The author obtruding 'himself' into the fictional action, like Alfred Hitchcock's hallmark cameos in his

movies, is by no means a new device. One of the fathers of
the English novel, Tobias Smollett, inserted himself slyly into
the narrative of *Humphry Clinker* (1771). The passage occurs
in a letter of Jeremy Melford's, dated 10 June, to Sir Watkins
Phillips. The (self-)portrait goes easy on the warts (and why
not? It is his novel):

> My curiosity being excited by this hint, I consulted my
> friend Dick Ivy, who undertook to gratify it the very next
> day, which was Sunday last. – He carried me to dine with
> S – , whom you and I have long known by his writings.
> He lives in the skirts of the town, and every Sunday his
> house is open to all unfortunate brothers of the quill,
> whom he treats with beef, pudding, and potatoes, port,
> punch, and Calvert's entire butt-beer. He has fixed upon
> the first day of the week for the exercise of his hospi-
> tality, because some of his guests could not enjoy it on
> any other, for reasons that I need not explain. I was civilly
> received, in a plain yet decent habitation, which opened
> backwards into a very pleasant garden, kept in excellent
> order; and, indeed, I saw none of the outward signs of
> authorship, either in the house or the landlord, who is
> one of those few writers of the age that stand upon their
> own foundation, without patronage, and above depend-
> ence. If there was nothing characteristic in the enter-
> tainer, the company made ample amends for his want
> of singularity.

Novelists evidently enjoy this game – like renaissance
painters, they sneak themselves in at the edges of their narratives. Malcolm Bradbury, for example, inserts the following
episode into his 1975 campus novel *The History Man*. The
ruthless seducing sociology lecturer, Howard Kirk has

tracked his sexual prey to the English department of Watermouth University:

> There is no response, so he knocks and waits again. The
> door of a room adjoining opens a little; a dark, tousled-
> haired head, with a sad visage, peers through, looks at
> Howard for a little, and then retreats. The face has a
> vague familiarity; Howard recalls that this depressed-
> looking figure is a lecturer in the English department, a
> man who, ten years earlier, had produced two tolerably
> well-known and acceptably reviewed novels, filled, as
> novels then were, with moral scruple and concern. Since
> then there has been silence, as if, under the pressure of
> contemporary change, there was no more moral scruple
> and concern, no new substance to be spun. The man
> alone persists; he passes nervously through the campus,
> he teaches sadly, he avoids strangers.

This, of course, is none other than Professor Malcolm Bradbury
of the University of East Anglia (a.k.a. Watermouth), famous
for his mop of tousled hair and his costive habit, in his prime,
of producing a novel only once every ten years. Bradbury was
also in his fiction a connoisseur of his age's moral exhaus-
tion. Bradbury, for his own ironic purposes (rather like Hitchcock's marginal irruption into his movies), has inserted into
his design a portrait of the artist as an old grump.

The first author to go whole hog with the author/hero
amalgam was, I believe, J. G. Ballard in *Crash* (1973), a violent
fantasia about the sexual pathology of automobile accidents.
Any resemblance between 'James Ballard', the hero narrator
of *Crash* and J. G. Ballard, the author of *Crash*, is – as novels
routinely (and unconvincingly) protest – 'accidental'. But
every reader will feel that what Ballard is doing with 'Ballard'

somehow goes against the rules of the game – as if a player picked up the soccer ball, threw it into the goal and waited to be embraced by his team mates. It is unsettling.

Ballard meant to unsettle us. He explained what he was doing in *Crash* in a 1995 preface to the novel:

> I feel that the balance between fiction and reality has changed significantly in the past decades. Increasingly their roles are reversed. We live in a world ruled by fictions of every kind – mass merchandizing, advertising, the pre-empting of any original response to experience by the television screen. We live inside an enormous novel.

Ellis's epigraph to *Lunar Park* makes a similar point: 'The occupational hazard of making a spectacle of yourself, over the long haul, is that at some point you buy a ticket too.' If, that is, you live inside enormous celebrity, you become the spectator of your own spectacle. Or, as the pungent idiom puts it, you start believing your own shit, and living it.

Genre bending, blending and fuzzy interpenetration need not be solemnly epistemological. Julian Barnes, for example, combines the belletristic essay with fiction in *Flaubert's Parrot* (1984) in which the narrative skims across the fact–fiction border like a flat stone skipping across the surface of a lake. (There was an interesting little spat between the novelist and the critic Christopher Ricks, who receives a side blast of personal names-named satire in *Flaubert's Parrot*.) Jonathan Safran Foer creates delicious comedy out of the device in *Everything is Illuminated*, the young American writer's triumphantly award-winning, 2002 bestselling first novel. It is, of course, a novel – as any shelf in Waterstone's or Borders (where it still sells like hot cakes) will testify.

Foer's story is simple. A young Jewish boy (Foer, that is) in New York discovers a photograph. His grandfather Safran, 'Jonathan' learns, was enabled to escape certain death in the Soviet Union in the Second World War by a heroic Russian woman. He undertakes a pilgrimage to the former Soviet Union to find out more about her. He is meanwhile writing a novel about his family's history, from the eighteenth century onwards, parts of which make up this novel. Another strand of *Everything is Illuminated* is the journal of his linguistically challenged translator, Alex (who will also, as the novel unfolds, discover unsettling things about his grandfather). The young Foer is (or, perhaps, not) the pivot around which the novel revolves. This is how Alex describes the young American, who is Alex's author as well as his client, on his arrival in the Ukraine:

> I was very flabbergasted by his appearance. This is an American? I thought. And also, This is a Jew? He was severely short. He wore spectacles and had diminutive hairs which were not split anywhere, but rested on his head like a Shapka ... He did not appear like either the Americans I had witnessed in magazines, with yellow hairs and muscles, or the Jews from history books, with no hairs and prominent bones.

Author photographs confirm that this is, linguistic lapses aside, a correct description of Mr Foer. There is no authorial photograph of Alex, of course, because he is not real. He and 'Jonathan', who are in some sense collaborating on the narrative, agree to change 'He was severely short' to 'Like me, he was not tall'. It is not changed in the text of *Everything is Illuminated*. The mind whirls.

The film of *Everything is Illuminated* was released in late 2005. Alas, the part of 'Foer' was not played by Foer but by Elijah Wood. As cast, and made up for his part, neither was he severely short nor did he have diminutive hairs. Which may account for the film's relative failure at the box office.

While the film was sinking at the box office, James Frey, the author of the 2003 confessional drunkalog *A Million Little Pieces*, was boosted into supersellerdom by endorsement from Oprah and inclusion in her book club list. Alas, investigative work by the Smoking Gun website revealed much of Mr Frey's memoir to be a tissue of – to be generous – 'fiction'. The luckless author (novelist?) was coerced into making a supplementary, and less remunerative confession on *Larry King Live*. His book, he claimed, was 'essentially true' although 'I changed things'. What novelist would not say the same?

We are, in general, more tolerant of the novel which in fact is essentially, or in some important way, autobiographical than we are of the autobiography which, like Frey's, takes unwarranted liberties with the facts. No one, for example, holds it against Zora Neale Hurston's *Dust Tracks on a Road* (1924), Kate Chopin's *The Awakening* (1899) or Maxine Hong Kingston's *The Woman Warrior* (1976) that they blend or bend genre. If anything, the *bona fides* of these works seem strengthened. Miles Franklin's prefatory statement on her novel (?) autobiography (?) *My Brilliant Career* (1901) is relevant:

MY DEAR FELLOW AUSTRALIANS

Just a few lines to tell you that this story is all about myself – for no other purpose do I write it.

I make no apologies for being egotistical. In this particular I attempt an improvement on other autobiographies. Other autobiographies weary one with excuses for their egotism. What matters it to you if I am egotistical? What matters it to you, though it should matter that I am not egotistical.

This is not a romance – I have too often faced the music of life to the tune of hardship to waste time in snivelling and gushing over fancies and dreams; neither is it a novel, but simply a yarn – a *real* yarn. Oh! As real, as really real – provided life itself is anything beyond a heartless little chimera – it is as real in its weariness and bitter heartache as the tall gum-trees, among which I first saw the light, are real in their stateliness and substantiality.

The moral for the wideawake novel user, is, know where the boundaries are and what games are being played; otherwise, when you find out, you will feel as foolish as those readers who think Harry Flashman was a historically real Victorian hero. 'Are you telling me *Lunar Park* isn't autobiographical?'

chapter 21

When worlds collide

FICTION HAS ITS fictional licence. When it wants to, the novel can play fast and loose with fact without doing itself mortal damage. The transgressions can, on occasion, however, confuse, delude or tantalise the reader. Take, for example, the following passage from Zadie Smith's *On Beauty*. The situation is, in plot terms, important. It is the funeral of Carlene Kipps, the Forsterian Mrs Wilcox figure. She is interred in the Victorian cemetery at Kensal Green. The section begins, 'The Victorians were terrific cemetery designers'. Zora Belsey, one of the younger mourners, is curious about the place:

> They kept their eyes to the ground and tried to walk at the proper funereal pace. The sun was so low that the stone crosses on one line of graves cast their spectral shadows on the plots of graves in front of them. In her hand Zora held a little leaflet she'd taken out of a box at the entrance. It featured an incomprehensible map of the

cemetery and a list of the notable dead. Zora was interested in seeking out Iris Murdoch or Wilkie Collins or Thackeray or Trollope or any of the other artists who, as the poet put it, went to paradise by way of Kensal Green.

Most readers will pass by the passage without their enjoyment of the novel being in the slightest troubled. But for those who have read, and recall, Peter J. Conradi's authoritative life of Iris Murdoch, the detail jars. The novelist's body does not lie at rest in the north London cemetery. Terminally ill with Alzheimer's disease, Murdoch was put into care in her last months:

> Gloria Richardson researched and found a nursing home, The Vale, in Oxford, where Iris with a teddy bear she named Jimbo felt at home. and where she died on Monday, 8 February 1999, at four in the afternoon. On television that night news of her death preceded that of King Hussein of Jordan and the latest difficulties of President Clinton. Like many in the last stages of her affliction, she had declined food and drink for some time. Her brain was donated to Optima. At her own request, none attended her cremation; nor the scattering of her ashes 'North of J8 flower-bed', as the undertakers vouchsafed, at Oxford Crematorium; and no memorial service followed.

How, then, should we read what Smith writes in her novel? As an ignorance on the part of the character, or a lapse by the author and her editor? Or 'no big deal, it's a novel, after all'?

However insignificant in the larger fictional scheme of things, such slips can be unsettling. But sometimes novelists want to unsettle us – to 'alienate' readers, as the Brechtian critics put it – so that we are jolted into realising that what we are reading is fiction. And, even if they do not deliberately intend to do such things, a slip such as Smith's has the same effect: keeping the reader on their toes. Take the following example from Douglas Adams's *So Long and Thanks for All the Fish* (1984), the fourth part of a trilogy [sic] dealing with Arthur Dent's aimless bouncing about the Milky Way. In quest of 'God's final message to his creation', Arthur and his girlfriend Fenchurch drop off for a brief tourist break in contemporary Los Angeles. They hire a car and cruise the freeways and boulevards:

Late in the evening they drove through Hollywood hills along Mulholland Drive and stopped to look out first over the dazzling sea of floating light that is Los Angeles, and later stopped to look across the dazzling sea of floating light that is the San Fernando Valley. They agreed that the sense of dazzle stopped immediately at the back of their eyes and didn't touch any other part of them and came away strangely unsatisfied by the spectacle. As dramatic seas of life went, it was fine, but light is meant to illuminate something, and having driven through what this particularly dramatic sea of light was illuminating they didn't think that much of it.

They slept late and restlessly and awoke at lunchtime when it was stupidly hot.

They drove out along the freeway to Santa Monica for their first look at the Pacific Ocean ... Their mood gradually lifted as they walked along the beach in Malibu and watched all the millionaires in their chic shanty huts carefully keeping an eye on each other to check out how rich they were each getting.

Their mood lifted further as the sun began to move down the western half of the sky, and by the time they

were back in their rattling car and driving towards a
sunset that no one of any sensibility would dream of
building Los Angeles in front of, they were suddenly
feeling astonishingly and irrationally happy and didn't
even mind that the terrible old car radio would only play
two stations, and those simultaneously. They were both
playing good rock and roll.[25]

The problem here is that if, starting from Malibu, you drive
as Arthur and Fenchurch evidently do down the Pacific
Coast Highway to Santa Monica then along the I-10 Freeway
to downtown Los Angeles, the sun is directly behind you,
sinking magnificently into the Pacific Ocean on 300 days a
year. In other words, as Dent and Fenchurch are placed, if
you drive 'towards' the sunset it would make better sense
to rent a submarine than a limousine. Since the *Hitchhiker*
series is a whimsical exercise in science fiction, it may be that
Adams's characters have found themselves in an 'alternative universe' in which the motion of the planets is reversed,
as time's arrow is supposed to be reversed at the other end
of black holes. Dedicated admirers of Adams may perhaps
see the error as cunningly designed to display Arthur Dent's
endearing provincialism. He is like the package tourist who
puts his holiday snaps the wrong way round in the projector
and does not notice. Nor, if we are good natured, do we. More
likely, of course, is that it is an authorial lapse.

In general, fiction has tightened up on its licence. Even in
sf, a genre to which Adams can claim part-time membership,
many writers, such as Brian Aldiss, have taken a self-denying
ordinance against the scientific nonsense of 'FTL' – faster than
light and time travel.[26] But in reading a novel like Adams's, we
allow him rather more slack because it is not hard sf, like

Arthur C. Clarke's, for example, but borderline 'fantasy'. We no more question the geography of Arthur Dent's toolings along the freeways of Southern California than the physics of quidditch in the Harry Potter series.

Historical fiction routinely commits terrible violations; no practitioner more so than the father of the genre, Walter Scott. With his novel *Kenilworth* (published in 1821 to coincide with the coronation of his fat friend George IV) Scott founded what was to become a Victorian industry, the lusty Elizabethan romance. Scott's novel popularised the Elizabethan age by presenting a set of tableaux which have entered folklore, where, thanks to Hollywood's and British television's enthusiastic revivals, they still have currency. These include Raleigh hurling down his cloak into the mud for his monarch to tread on, thereby earning himself a knighthood. The story is, of course, apocryphal. And *Kenilworth* is shot through with heroic anachronism. Shakespeare is given a walk-on part (historically, he was eleven at the time) and characters quote from one of his last plays, *The Tempest*. The novel would fail any GCSE history test. And yet it has done more to frame posterity's idea of the Elizabethan age than any work of either fiction or non-fiction before or since.

So who should the reader trust, Sir Walter Scott, wizard of the north, or David Starkey, the superdon and television presenter, who as I write, is currently thundering against some wretched re-creation of Elizabeth's reign, in the style of Scott? In an ideal world, I would like to suggest, a mixture of the two (Scottkey?) should be used self-correctingly, and for the mutual illumination they provide. Take, as a more recent example, the most lauded American novel of 2005–6, E. L. Doctorow's *The March*. Doctorow's narrative chronicles General William Tecumseh Sherman's ferocious incursion during the American Civil War into the southern states, burning, plundering, fighting his way to the heart of Secession. The event is etched, melodramatically, on the public sensibility by one of the all-time favourite films, *Gone with the Wind*, and the image of Scarlett, the Southern Belle agonistes, standing against a burning Atlanta.

Doctorow's novel focuses, unromantically, on the camp followers: the field hospital workers, the deserters, the civilian casualties – above all, on the ragtag army of 25,000 'freed' (that is, dispossessed) slaves, dragged along in the vortex of Sherman's Blitzkrieg. The imagery evokes the 'liberation' of Iraq (particularly the disruption left in the wake of the spring 2003 'dash to Baghdad') and, even more topically, the thousands of dispossessed and wholly disoriented African-Americans huddling in the Superdome after Katrina's assault on New Orleans. The 'she' in the following passage is a former slave, Pearl, pale enough – by virtue of miscegenation – to pass for white. Pearl has been adopted as a mascot by Sherman and, surely, was conceived by Doctorow as a kind of antitype, chromatically and racially, to Scarlett:

> Moments later she was flying down the stairs in her bare feet. She let herself out the front door and headed across the road and into the pasture, where, in the distance, the blacks were camped. She could see everything clear in the moonlight, the rises and dips in the earth, the paled leaves of grass, the lean-tos and wagons up ahead, and the embers of the cook fires glowing like stars in the fields. Ten minutes later she was walking in the paths of this improvised settlement, and many people were awake, huddled in their blankets around their fires, or rocking infants in their arms, or simply standing by their rigs and wagons and staring at her as she passed by. In their eyes

she was a white woman, an army woman, and if they were curious as to what she was doing among them they did not demean themselves to inquire. They were being sent off to walk by themselves in the direction prescribed for them by their hero and saviour, General Sherman. All they had wanted to do was praise him, revere him, and now he was turning them away, sending them off on their own, and what their destination was or what would happen to them when they got there nobody knew.

The principal character in *The March* is Sherman himself – but is the image of him, his military strategy and the last, terrible months of the conflict supplied by Doctorow's fiction 'truer' than that given in Ken Burns's hugely successful PBS documentary about the Civil War, serialised in 1990? Is the image of Churchill offered by Michael Dobbs's current biofictional multi-volume saga 'truer' than Martin Gilbert's authorised multi-volume biography? Was Dickens's *A Tale of Two Cities* truer than 'Mr Carlyle's wonderful book' (*The French Revolution*) on which it was based? Is Susan Sontag's 1992 revisionist depiction of Nelson in *The Volcano Lovers* a truer portrayal of the victor of Trafalgar than the heroic-romantic versions that were trafficked in his anniversary year of 2005, or is it mere novelistic perversion? Who is right – the novelist or the historian? Or is it a category error even to ask such questions?

The answer is that the two kinds of discourse are not in direct competition. Fiction can claim that it is particularly good at depicting the 'fuzziness' of history, its refusal to fall into satisfactory shapes and clear-line patterns. It is both contradictory and complementary. Its 'licence' allows it to stretch history, find break points, look at events from different angles and, more often than not, take unwarranted liberties in doing so. But, even at its most wrong, it is usually more readable than historical chronicle. And, of course, because it is 'fiction', sensible readers (not, alas, always a majority) do not take a novel as the last word on anything.

Arguably, fiction – with its unique ability to 'extend sympathy', in George Eliot's phrase – can deliver a different but equally valuable kind of knowledge. A few years ago, the A-level examining boards in Britain introduced for those pupils studying the Humanities what were called 'synoptic' papers. One such, very popular with English Literature candidates, was a paper based on the Great War. For me, interviewing applicants to university who had taken the option was illuminating. To a boy and girl, all had read, with delight and instruction, Sebastian Faulks's *Birdsong* (1993), and, almost as many, Pat Barker's *Regeneration* trilogy (1990–95). Ask them about the mechanics of 'sapping', the hardship of the trenches, the 'passive suffering' (as Yeats, rather offensively, called the subject matter of Wilfred Owen's poetry) and they were brilliant. Ask the same, clued-up pupils about the assassination of Franz Ferdinand or the Treaty of Versailles, or even when and why America entered the war, and you would be met, in most cases, with blank looks. They did not know. One kind of knowledge – that communicated by fiction – had, it seemed, blocked out the knowledge communicated by the traditional history lesson. But which knowledge, a hundred years on, is the more valuable to an 18-year old (the average age, of course, of the four million casualties in the First World War)?

Traffic across the historical–fictional border is, of course, two way. Selecting at random from today's newspapers as I write (Sunday, 11 December, 2005), I find the following headlines in the news section of the *Sunday Telegraph*:

FLYING SQUADS RESCUE HEARTS FROM DARKNESS
(The story is about a British charity doing good works in
Mozambique, the headline echoes Joseph Conrad's *Heart
of Darkness*.)

CAMERON IS NOT BRIDESHEAD REBRANDED
(A political comment piece by Matthew d'Ancona on
the new Conservative Party leader David Cameron. The
allusion is to Evelyn Waugh's *Brideshead Revisited*.)

and

IRAQ'S DR NO SAYS YES TO PEACE AND DEMOCRACY
(A story on changes of government policy in Iraq. The
allusion is to Ian Fleming's James Bond thriller.)

The *Observer* on the same day has the headline:

OUT OF THE COLD, ON TO THE WEB
(A story about MI5's archive being declassified and posted
on the world wide web. The allusion is to John Le Carré's
The Spy Who Came in from the Cold.)

It is probably not accidental that the three novelists alluded
to in the *Sunday Telegraph* are notably (in Waugh's case, fanati-
cally) Tory and that the *Observer*'s John Le Carré is radical left
in his political leaning.

More significant is how fiction, with its huge readerships and immediacy of impact, has created the context, or
map, within which these events are placed. Consciousness
of Africa, the Third World and the murky goings on of international espionage has, for most of the population, been
framed by the fiction they read. Edgar Wallace supplies a

useful example. 'The King of the Thrillers' visited the Belgian Congo in 1907 and, like Joseph Conrad, was appalled by what he saw. On his return, as a stalwart of the London branch of the Congo Reform Association, he resolved to write a novel outlining what an ideal imperial administration (that is, as unlike the rapacities of King Leopold's Congo as possible) should be like. The result was *Sanders of the River* (1910). As devised by Wallace, Mr Commissioner Sanders is a grey-haired, yellow-faced wise old bird who has been 'called upon by the British government to keep a watchful eye upon some quarter of a million cannibal folk' – a task which he carries out with shrewd and often draconian efficiency. The Sanders stories all centre on stern and arbitrary acts of 'justice', which the commissioner jovially administers with the assistance of his steamboat, his Houssa police and, above all, his Maxim gun.

The stories were immensely popular at the time and *Sanders of the River* was filmed in 1935, with the American Marxist Paul Robeson playing Bosambo and the future first president of Kenya, Jomo Kenyatta, an uncredited extra among all the other cannibal folk. Four years later, the juvenile Martin Luther King appeared, skipping and singing, as a 'piccaninny' in a stage prologue to the first showing of the movie *Gone with the Wind* at the Egyptian cinema in Atlanta. A colourful event, apparently. (Only whites, of course, were allowed in the opening night audience. 'No Coloreds'.)

The reconditioning of western views of Africa has many cultural and educational sources, but not least are novels such as Alan Paton's *Cry, the Beloved Country* (1948) – a reverse shot of South Africa from the viewpoint of the oppressed – not jovial (Bo)sambos or piccaninnies, but real, suffering people. Paton's novel was potent armament in the eventual overthrow of apartheid, a regime which, although not identified by that name, was staunchly believed in and enforced by Sanders of the River.

Yet another, and much more recent spin on the west's Africa problem was given by the bestselling-novel film tie-in of John Le Carré's *The Constant Gardener* (2001), a fiction which, with a kind of 'plague on both your houses' analysis, depicts via 'Big Pharma' the developed world's cynical exploitation of Africa, specifically Kenya, and Africa's apparently ineradicable political corruption.

Whether or not novels are historically accurate (historians invariably reject or qualify their depictions), there is no questioning their power to form received historical and social thinking. It was a power politely acknowledged by Abraham Lincoln, on meeting Harriet Beecher Stowe, author of *Uncle Tom's Cabin* (1851): 'So this is the little lady who started a great war.' Honest Abe's sentiment could have been echoed by Tony Blair, were he ever brave enough to be seen publicly in the company of the author of *The Satanic Verses*: 'So this is the man who provoked the greatest crisis in Anglo-Iranian relations since the fall of Mossadeg, and whose book presaged the twenty-first-century clash of civilisations.' Dream on.

chapter 22

Fiction – where the unspeakable can be spoken

AS THE RUSHDIE example suggests, history is not merely something made and stored in the past. It is happening all around us, and the novel, with its finger on the socio-historical pulse, can be intimately involved. There are any number of possible answers to the question 'Why read novels'? – a question which all dedicated novel readers will face from time to time.

The one-word answer which is most likely to slap down facile objections of the 'what a waste of time' variety is, in some novels at least: 'race'. Take, for example, the surprise 2004 winner of both the Whitbread prize and the Orange prize, Andrea Levy's *Small Island*. Literary quality aside, fiction like Levy's, alas, is the only place nowadays where you are likely to find any grown-up discussion of race. In America, a parallel discussion of the elsewhere *undiscussable* topic (as Henry James would have put it) is conducted by writers such as Tom Wolfe (in, for example, *The Bonfire of the Vanities* (1987)), Philip Roth (*The Human Stain* (2000)) and Toni Morrison

Inside, the novel is more enlightened

(*Beloved*). Outside fiction, race is such a hot-button issue that politicians and press will handle it only with pious platitudes and hobbled correctness.

Andrea Levy has obvious qualifications, other than her belatedly recognised talent, to join in the grown-up British debate on race. A young-middle-aged Briton of colour, she cannot remember the first, post-Windrush generation of Jamaican immigrants that her narrative deals with. But she can doubtless recall the 'No coloureds' cards put up by landlords in newsagents' windows. She can certainly remember Enoch Powell's 1968 'Rivers of Blood' speech, to which she alluded in her prize-acceptance speeches. She would have been one of those 'piccaninnies' the politician referred to.

I personally, like others of my generation, owe some initial instruction about the realities of race in Britain to Colin MacInnes's 1957 novel *City of Spades*. Ignore the racist banalities on the paperback cover – interestingly reflective as they are of the unreconstructed attitudes of the time. With the acuity of the accomplished novelist, MacInnes was far ahead of the newspapers, the pundits, his publishers and the bigot in the street (then virtually every white-skinned person). MacInnes caught precisely the perverse nature of British prejudice as it was applied in the 1950s. As one of his black characters describes it: 'Universal politeness, and universal coldness. Few love us, few hate us, but everybody wishes we are not here, and shows this to us by the correct standaway behaviour that is your great English secret.'

Despite the decade's cultural emancipations, little changes fundamentally in the 1960s. There is a matching scene in *Small Island* where the hero, Gilbert, applies for a driver's job (something his time in the RAF had trained him for). He and the personnel manager get on famously, reminiscing about their time in the service. Finally Gilbert asks, 'Do I have the job?' No, his still-smiling interviewer tells him, 'You see, we have white women working here.' Stand away, Gilbert, if you would be so kind.

Small Island's winning of the Orange prize coincided, almost to the day, with Michael Howard, then leader of the opposition Tories, launching 'immigration' (euphemism for race) as his party's big theme as they approached the 2005 General Election (which they lost). Race has simmered in the US continuously over the last decades, with sporadic eruptions such as the Rodney King riots and the OJ and MJ court cases.

Newspapers, like politicians, touch the hot potato very nervously. Only the wholly unelectable, and wholly contemptible (Jean-Marie Le Pen, David Duke, the demagogues of the British National Party) play the race card. Novels, however, go where journos and politicos do not dare. Take, as a prime example, Philip Roth's *The Human Stain*. (If you haven't read the novel, or seen the film, register a spoiler alert and skip to the next section.) Roth's narrative picks up on the end-of-career story of Coleman Silk, a Jewish professor of classics at a small, elite eastern seaboard university, Athena – one of the so-called 'potted Ivy League' colleges. Silk was, as the novel puts it, 'one of a handful of Jews on the Athena faculty when he was hired [in the 1950s] and perhaps among the first of the Jews permitted to teach in a classics department anywhere in America'. The persistence of institutionalised prejudice in America is one of the country's better repressed memories. In the institution where I currently teach, on the West Coast, I still meet retired professors who can recall not being able to live in the vicinity of the university where they taught because the area was 'restricted' (that is, off limits to Jews and other undesirables).

Since the 1964 Civil Rights Act, the former discriminatory practices of such institutions of higher learning (no blacks, Jews only on a quota system) have been rolled back. In Roth's novel, it is now the late 1990s. But the bruises and raw spots, legacies of racism, survive, and suppurate poisonously – at least, in Roth's diagnosis. Condoleezza Rice may not agree.

Silk, on the verge of honourable retirement, comes into his class one day, halfway through a semester. As the narrative puts it:

> The class consisted of fourteen students. Coleman had taken attendance at the beginning of the first several lectures so as to learn their names. As there were still two names that failed to elicit a response by the fifth week into the semester, Coleman, in the sixth week, opened the session by asking 'Does anyone know these people? Do they exist or are they spooks?'

As it happens, the absentee pair are African-American students. They are underperforming, it emerges, in all their classes – those classes that they bother to attend. The clear implication is that they have only gained entrance to this élite institution by virtue of affirmative action so the college does not lose its federal funding on the grounds of discrimination. They should not be there.

Silk has made a monumentally (but unintentionally) inappropriate remark. By 'spooks' he meant, are they 'ghosts'? 'I had no idea what their colour might be', he later protests, when hauled up for that most heinous of offences, political incorrectness on matters of race. The luckless professor of classics does not know, or does not remember, that 'spook' is 'an invidious term also applied to blacks'. Unwittingly, he has publicly uttered something equivalent to: 'Are they lazy niggers?' He might as well have opened his fly and urinated over the front row of his class.

Complications inevitably ensue. Silk, with only months to serve in a distinguished career, is hounded out of the profession he has so nobly served. His wife dies under the strain and humiliation. At the fulcrum of the story comes Roth's bombshell surprise. Silk, it emerges, is not, after all, Jewish. Nor is he white gentile. He is a light-skinned African-American. At the pivotal moment of his early career young Coleman (the name suddenly takes on significance 'coal black man') had the choice of 1) becoming a professional boxer – something in which he excelled and for whose prizes, following the pioneering trails of the Brown Bomber, his race was newly eligible; or 2) taking advantage of his light skin to enter higher education as a tawny, curly-haired, too-clever-for-his-own-good Jew. He chose the second. His stainless skin made it possible. But was he, the novel inquires, denying his humanity by taking that option?

In *The Human Stain*, Roth confronts and anatomises the corruptions, as he conceives them, brought about by the over-liberal surrender by America to civil rights orthodoxies. There are many targets in this most polemical, and morally reckless, of novels. Roth lashes out right and left at what he sees as American hypocrisy. The blue-nosed brigade's attack on Clinton over his Lewinsky lapse particularly irritates him and the author devotes a furious prefatory chapter to the epidemic hypocrisy of the time. There should be, Roth whimsically suggests, 'a mammoth banner, draped dadaistically like a Christo wrapping from one end of the White House to the other bearing the legend A HUMAN BEING LIVES HERE'. And, by implication, another mammoth banner should be draped over the whole of the edifice of American higher education reading: 'HUMAN BEINGS TEACH HERE'.

The advantage of fiction, as Roth wields it, is that it need not pull its punches. Partly, of course, because no one takes it seriously, on the 'only a novel' principle. you do not, of course, have to agree with Roth any more than with Tom Wolfe in his brutal satire on the failures of black political leadership in America's metropolitan cities in *A Man in Full* (1998). But both novelists put the issues on the table.

There are many other hot-button issues which fiction fearlessly discusses: Islamic fundamentalism (*The Satanic Verses*), euthanasia (*Sons and Lovers*), paedophilia (Vladimir Nabokov's *Lolita* (1955), A. M. Homes's *The End of Alice* (1996), Gabriel Garcia Marquez's *Memories of My Melancholy Whores* (2004)). It is possible to mount any number of defences of fiction. But socio-historical relevance is one of the more hard-hitting.

chapter 23

I'm a Martian: will I understand
Pride and Prejudice?

THE MOST INFLUENTIAL, and attacked, fiction review
of 2005 was written by John Banville, who also, as it happens,
published one of the most applauded and derided novels of
2005. In the *New York Review of Books* (NYRB) of 26 May, 2005,
Banville undertook a critical demolition of Ian McEwan's
novel *Saturday*, which had come out in the United Kingdom
the previous January and was on the point of being released
in the United States.

McEwan's book had been enthusiastically received in
London – so enthusiastically that the bookmakers and book
trade prophets, early in the prize-awarding season as it was,
made it favourite to win the Man Booker in the autumn. In
fact, in the estimation of some, that bauble was too small an
award for McEwan – the Nobel, surely, was in prospect. This
expectation was confirmed by the novelist's being put on the
shortlist, along with previous Nobel Prize winners such as
Saul Bellow, for Man Booker's newly established, international, lifetime fiction award.

Buoyed up by its reception, and by its author's reputation, *Saturday* promptly shot into the UK bestseller list. The novel is circadian, covering the events of one Saturday in February 2003. For the main protagonist, Henry Perowne, it is, at least as the day dawns, the beginning of just another weekend in the life of a happily married, prosperous, professionally successful Londoner. On Saturday Henry enjoys his well-earned weekly break from his work as a brain surgeon. On this particular Saturday he plans to squeeze in a game of squash, do some shopping, make love to his wife (twice) and prepare for a family dinner party in the evening. The day turns out to be more eventful than was planned. Not just for Perowne, but for London. It is the day of the great 'Not in My Name' anti-Iraq War march.

Perowne, a politically disengaged man, is dimly aware of the demonstrators, initially as something that jams up the streets around his house, gym and fishmongers. Iraq presses obscurely on his consciousness. He is aware something is going on, but he has no clear sympathy with the hundreds of thousands of people demonstrating – nor any great antipathy. As it unfolds, *Saturday* becomes complicated, violent and politically instructive for Henry Perowne. Sunday will find him a very different man.

The London reviewers, including myself, loved *Saturday*. Banville, looking across the Atlantic (from New York, not his native Dublin), saw their unanimous hurrah as so much chauvinistic log-rolling. It was follow my leader. McEwan was a British star, and no one in his metropolitan galaxy was prepared to stand up and criticise. *Saturday*'s reception was symptomatic of a literary culture gone soft-minded with hype and nepotism.

Saturday was, Banville pronounced, 'a dismayingly bad book':

Another source of dismay, one for which, admittedly, Ian McEwan cannot be held wholly accountable, is the ecstatic reception which Saturday has received from reviewers and book buyers alike. Are we in the West so shaken in our sense of ourselves and our culture, are we so disablingly terrified in the face of the various fanaticisms which threaten us, that we can allow ourselves to be persuaded and comforted by such a self-satisfied and, in many ways, ridiculous novel as this?

At this stage there had been no American reviews other than Banville's. It was London, and its universal chorus of praise for Saturday that he was thinking of. Also the phrase 'not be held wholly accountable' suggested a degree of complicity on the author's part.

There was immediate protest. If you prick British reviewers they do not bleed, they kick. Savagely. Never, said Benjamin Franklin, pick a fight with a man carrying a barrel of ink. The British reviewing establishment had a tanker's-worth of the black stuff to throw. Banville, it was said, was jealous. He was a writer who had never enjoyed big sales, who had been to the Booker altar many times but had never won (unlike McEwan, who had won once and now, it seemed, would win again). The review was mediocrity's bile in the face of genius.

None the less, Banville's denunciation had a palpable impact. A bandwagon was halted. Is Saturday, it was asked, really that good? Backlash is too strong a word: but second thoughts were voiced. Very rarely does a review entirely reverse a tide of critical opinion. But, it seems, Banville may have stemmed the tide somewhat.

McEwan's novel, in the final analysis, did not make it to the Man Booker shortlist in October, whereas Banville's The Sea did, of course, and won. There were those, late in 2005, who saw Banville's review as having been a kind of sabotage, a disgracefully low-minded pre-emptive strike. Craig Raine, who is one of the author's friends, acknowledged in Saturday, doing his annual round-up of best books of the year for The Times Literary Supplement, was outright, echoing what was, by December, the orthodoxy among the McEwanite faction:

> Ian McEwan's Saturday should have won this year's Booker Prize. It was harmed by two things – envy and envy. After the novel's catastrophic Royal Flush of laudatory reviews, John Banville's notice in the New York Review of Books spoke to, and for, every disconcerted rival pained by mention of the Nobel Prize. It was an extra irony that Banville's novel should carry off the discredited prize. McEwan's novel isn't perfect, but it has bravura evocations (perhaps a couple too many) of surgical operations that are unrivalled in fiction. The happy family of the surgeon is a little too implausibly gifted, but the meticulous formal organization of the novel around the theme of brain damage is elegant and Euclidean. Banville's damaging review was a coarse caricature.

Without either joining in the critical fray, which continued well into 2006, or taking sides, I must inquire how competently Banville could have read Saturday. Was he, on the evidence of his review, equipped to pronounce so pontifically ('dismayingly bad book') and, as Raine witnesses, so 'damagingly'? In fact, as I wrote to the NYRB at the time, a central point in Banville's review depends on what looks like a gross misreading of the text. There is, in the opening section of Saturday's narrative, a 17-page, ball-by-ball description of a squash match. It is one of many extended set pieces on which the narrative hinges. Perowne might have won, but on the way to the gym he is involved in a car crash and is beaten up by a thug who is to invade his home later that night. Distracted by the violence, Perowne narrowly loses to his rival on a dubious let point. The loss hovers, meaningfully, over the whole novel. Things are going wrong, the Saturday routine is disturbed. Banville, however, repeatedly asserts in his review that Perowne won the squash match. In reply to my letter pointing out the error, he retorted:

> Summoned, one shuffles guiltily into the Department of Trivia. I have no knowledge of, and care nothing for, the game of squash. Having read Ian McEwan's description of the match between Perowne and his American friend, all seventeen pages of it, I formed the notion that after a shaky start, and despite his experiences in the morning – traffic accident, encounter with thug, punch in the chest, etc. – Perowne managed to outplay his opponent who, however, deprived him of what he clearly considered a victory by demanding a let or somesuch – as I say, I am ignorant in these matters, and McEwan's account of the game made me no wiser, due no doubt to my sluggish comprehension rather than his powers of description.

For all the huffpuff, it is a convincing answer. Banville does not understand the game of squash. He did not go to an English public school. He is not English, for God's sake. I have often felt the same way about baseball – as portrayed in a novel like Bernard Malamud's *The Natural* (1952), for example. But does the error not indicate a disabling alienation from the 'world' of the novel, more particularly the lifestyle of a top London surgeon?

Although it did not emerge in this little spat, there are other examples of disabling cultural blind spots in the review.

Describing what he saw as Perowne's nauseating uxorious-
ness, Banville wrote:

> Throughout their marriage he has never strayed once, nor
> has he wished to – 'What a stroke of luck, that the woman
> he loves is also his wife' – and why would he, since she
> is a paragon, beautiful, clever, sympathetic, and wise ...
> Apparently in the purlieus of north London, or at least in
> McEwan's fantasy version of them, no one suffers from
> morning breath, and women long-married wake up every
> time primed for sex – as the book ends, no one will be
> surprised to learn, there is another amatory encounter
> between husband and wife.

North London! The action of *Saturday* is circumscribed
within an area, around six hundred yards in diameter, of WC1
– West Central London, on the fringe of raffish Fitzrovia and
genteel Bloomsbury. The epicentre of the novel is Fitzroy
Square, where McEwan himself lives. The square (like
Gordon Square, a little to the east, in Bloomsbury) has a blue
plaque indicating that Virginia Woolf lived there. The topog-
raphy of *Saturday* is as tight, precise and integral to the plot
as its circadian time frame. So topographically precise is the
narrative that one can pace it out like a football pitch (two
hundred yards from Fitzroy Square to Maple Street, three
hundred yards across Maple Street to University Street, fifty
yards to Gower Street and Huntley Street, five hundred yards
in the other direction to Marylebone High Street).

If you know central London, the novel has a distinct
Fitzrovian feel to it. North London is Islington, Blairland.
It has a quite different feel. This is not a North London
novel. Nick Hornby's fiction is. Hanif Kureishi's *The Buddha
of Suburbia* (1990) is quintessentially 'Sarf' London. Tim

McEwan's Fitzroy Square

Lott's *White City Blue* (1999) is quintessentially West London, round Shepherd's Bush and the uneasy terrain between W6 and W8. Russell Hoban's *Angelica's Grotto* (1999) is quintessentially Temple and Strand. Peter Ackroyd's *The Great Fire of London* (1982) is the area around the old Marshalsea prison, Jake Arnott's *The Long Firm* trilogy belongs in Soho's naughty square mile. The list could be extended through all points of the London A to Z. The point is, there are many Londons in London fiction. And *Saturday* is a quintessentially Fitzrovia–Bloomsbury novel.

Not to have picked up on reverberations of location in *Saturday* is to be radically at odds with McEwan's novel. It is the equivalent of having Sherman McCoy in *The Bonfire of the Vanities* live in the Bronx and lose his way in Manhattan, rather than the other way round. What would Banville have replied, had he been presented with this objection? 'I have no knowledge of, and care nothing for, the city of London'? But to admit such a thing would be, arguably, to disqualify yourself from pronouncing authoritatively on a novel as wholly immersed in its urban setting as *Ulysses* is in the city of Dublin, or Alfred Döblin's *Berlin Alexanderplatz* (1929) in that city.

It raises the question – if you really want to get into and on top of a novel – do you have to be intimately knowledgeable about the world in which it is set? Within reason, yes. It helps. The principle can, of course, be carried too far. In the post-Banvillean *Saturday fracas* can be heard some truly piddling objections. When Perowne bumps his assailants' BMW with his Mercedes, they are lurching out of the Spearmint Rhino on Tottenham Court Road. That gentlemen's club (it is precisely where McEwan says it is, at the junction with University Street) is not, as it happens, open in the small hours of

Saturday morning. The model of the expensive Mercedes saloon which Perowne is driving does not, as McEwan's narrative describes it, have manual stick-shift gears. It is an automatic. From which it can be deduced that novelists, even novelists as successful as McEwan, do not hang out in night clubs and drive expensive saloon cars home after the lap-dancing is over. The gym to which, identifiably, Perowne is driving (Fitness Exchange in Huntley Street) does not have a squash court. Presumably McEwan plays elsewhere.

Do such 'errors' matter? No – unless you have the readerly equivalent of Obsessive Compulsive Disorder. Do Banville's blunders about squash and WC1 matter? Arguably they might.

Craig Raine, McEwan's defender quoted above, is the acknowledged founder and lead exponent of what became known in the 1970s as the 'Martian School' of poetry (a piece of which is quoted, with Raine's permission, in Saturday – who says the London literary world does not hang out together?) The Martian School took off from a squib by Raine's friend, Martin Amis, and was given its label by Raine's much reprinted volume of poetry, A Martian Sends a Postcard Home (1979). The central, rather jokey idea is that visiting Martians – 'beings', as H. G. Wells puts it, 'with intellects infinitely superior to ours' – can observe earthlings very precisely, but cannot for the life of them understand what the earthlings are actually doing. This, for example, is how the Martian makes sense of the telephone:

In homes, a haunted apparatus sleeps,
that snores when you pick it up.

If the ghost cries, they carry it
to their lips and soothe it to sleep

with sounds. And yet they wake it up
deliberately, by tickling with a finger.

The Martian poems are ingenious exercises in defamil-
iarisation. But there is, of course, a touch of the Martian in
most readers of most novels. I may know what a telephone is,
but do I really, for all the Victorian fiction I have read, know
what Dickens's London was like? What, with all those tons
of horse manure and worse tipped on to its streets daily, it
smelled like? What, before modern domestic sanitation,
Londoners themselves smelled like? Can I really put together
in my mind, in anything but the sketchiest way, the French
provincial milieu which drives Emma Bovary to distraction, or
Anna Karenina's Moscow, or even Irvine Welsh's Edinburgh?
Muriel Spark's and even Ian Rankin's Edinburgh I feel more
confident about, having lived a middle-class existence in the
city for ten years.

The more familiar or 'inward' you are with a novel's
world, the subtler your understanding of the novel. To put it
another way, the less Martian you are about it, the less likely
you are to make slips such as John Banville's. But I cannot be
doctrinaire on the point. Take, for example, the contrary case
of Michael Cunningham and Virginia Woolf. Although not as
far away as Mars, the Los Angeles suburb of La Cañada, where
Cunningham was brought up, is a long way from Woolfland,
the leafy squares of Bloomsbury and Fitzrovia.

La Cañada Flintridge, to give it its full name, nestles under
the San Gabriel hills, along the 210 Freeway, in one of the two
great canyon systems that branch out from L. A. La Cañada is
dry, dusty and, as the smog barrels along the valleys driven
by the afternoon onshore winds, not a good place to be if you
have pulmonary ailments.[27] But it has good schools, having,

unlike neighbouring Pasadena, opted out from the bussing reforms of the 1960s. Aspiring parents pay above the odds for houses there. How, then, did a kid from this southern California backwater become the most admired Woolfian of the 1990s, with his Pulitzer Prize-winning novel The Hours and the subsequent, Oscar-winning film? This is how Cunningham himself explains it in an interview he gave to www.powells.com in June 2005:

> I was drifting along at fifteen in La Cañada High School, sneaking a cigarette one day, trying to look dangerous, when I found myself standing next to the pirate queen of the entire school. (These were the '60s, when the poor teachers, desperate to look cool, had us analyzing rock lyrics.) She was beautiful and smart, dressed in the skins of the animals she'd slain, and I was desperate to impress her. I mentioned Leonard Cohen. 'Have you ever thought of being less stupid?' she said and gave me a copy of Mrs Dalloway.

Did he find it difficult – 'alien'? Cunningham was asked:

> It was opaque to me. I wasn't so young and stupid that I couldn't see the balance of those sentences. I was like an aborigine hearing Beethoven. She was doing with language what Jimi Hendrix was doing with music, recklessly flirting with chaos. It wasn't until I read Mrs Dalloway that I saw what you could do with language, that I saw that it could be as vital and alive as rock and roll, which is what I had really been interested in.

Cunningham paid off his debt to Woolf with The Hours (Woolf's working title for Mrs Dalloway). It is a complicated fantasia on Woolf's novel , moving between 1920s London, 1940s Los Angeles and 1990s New York – each time setting with its version of the Woolfian archetypal heroine and Bloomsbury resonances. Cunningham takes as his epigraph the following August 1923 entry from Woolf's diary:

> I have no time to describe my plans. I should say a good deal about The Hours, & my discovery; how I dig out beautiful caves behind my characters.

Cunningham, too, digs out his beautiful caves behind Woolf's characters. Take the following passage from Mrs Dalloway, in which Clarissa is buying the flowers for her party that evening from Mulberry's in Bond Street. As she makes her choice, with the assistant Miss Pym, there is a loud bang:

> The violent explosion which made Mrs Dalloway jump and Miss Pym go to the window and apologise came from a motor car which had drawn to the side of the pavement precisely opposite Mulberry's shop window. Passers-by who, of course, stopped and stared, had just time to see a face of the very greatest importance against the dove-grey upholstery, before a male hand drew the blind and there was nothing to be seen except a square of dove grey.
>
> Yet rumours were at once in circulation from the middle of Bond Street to Oxford Street on one side, to Atkinson's scent shop on the other, passing invisibly, inaudibly, like a cloud, swift, veil-like upon hills, falling indeed with something of a cloud's sudden sobriety and stillness upon faces which a second before had been utterly disorderly. But now mystery had brushed them with her wing; they had heard the voice of authority; the spirit of religion was abroad with her eyes bandaged tight

and her lips gaping wide. But nobody knew whose face had been seen. Was it the Prince of Wales's, the Queen's, the Prime Minister's? Whose face was it? Nobody knew.

This is how the scene is transmuted in Cunningham's adaptation. Clarissa, in smart 1990s Manhattan, comes out of a shop bearing flowers. A small knot of people are gathered around, not a taxi but a film-shoot trailer:

> Clarissa positions herself beside two young girls, one with hair dyed canary yellow and the other with hair dyed platinum. Clarissa wonders if they intended so strongly to suggest the sun and the moon.
>
> Sun says to Moon, 'It was Meryl Streep, definitely Meryl Streep.'
>
> Clarissa is excited despite herself. She was right. There is a surprisingly potent satisfaction in knowing that her vision was shared by another.
>
> 'No way,' says Moon. 'It was Susan Sarandon'.
>
> It was not, Clarissa thinks, Susan Sarandon. It may have been Vanessa Redgrave but it was certainly not Susan Sarandon.
>
> 'No,' says Sun, 'it was Streep. Trust me.'
>
> 'It was not Meryl Streep.'
>
> 'It was. It fucking was.'

To get the most out of this passage requires a daunting range of intertextual reference. The actress Meryl Streep plays Clarissa Vaughan (the observer here) in the 2002 movie of *The Hours*. Vanessa Redgrave played Clarissa Dalloway in the (appalling) 1997 film adaptation of Woolf's novel. But it is Cunningham's artful echoing of the narrative of *Mrs Dalloway* which is central. *The Hours* would be a very thin experience for the visiting Martian, however advanced its reading skills.

What is most astonishing, however, is the familiarity or 'inwardness' which Cunningham – brought up a continent and over half a century away – achieves with the London and England of Virginia Woolf. There are occasional lapses of authenticity (he calls 'railway stations' 'rail stations' and 'drawing rooms' 'parlors', for example). But in general, the evocation is pitch perfect. It is very reassuring. It can be done. It is possible to reach across time and space to converse, intelligently, with Tolstoy, Sterne, Thomas Mann, Nick Hornby – or even Ian McEwan. Not only can authors do it, but readers can as well. There is hope for the Martian reader yet.

chapter 24

Can reviews help?

IN ORDER TO make full use of reviews it is helpful to know something about the history of reviewing. There were books centuries before there were book reviews and, quite likely, there will be books afterwards. At the moment the book-buying public of the United Kingdom has a lot of reviews thrown at it. Unlike other advanced literary cultures (America, France, Italy) the London-based press hosts a unique profusion of mass readership reviewing outlets. No other country has a dozen national, as opposed to metropolitan, regional or city, newspapers with weekly literary supplements, from the Daily Mail, in ascending height of brow, to the Guardian.

Add to that output the Sundays, the political weeklies, and the two heavies, The Times Literary Supplement (TLS) and the London Review of Books (LRB) and noteworthy authors can hope for up to twenty, often conflicting opinions passed on their book the moment it hits the high street bookstores. Who knows? They may even see it slathered with royal jelly in the Saturday Telegraph and doused in an acid bath of critical scorn the next day in the *Sunday Telegraph*. Such are the fortunes of British novelists.

Inevitably, with so many hands to it, the net is spread wide. More books are reviewed for more would-be readers in the London press than in any other capital city. New York has *The New York Times Book Review*, the *New York Review of Books*, some few pages in the *Village Voice*, and what else?[28]

'Reviewing' as we know it began in the early nineteenth century with 'big bow-wow' magazines like the *Edinburgh Review* (Whig) and the *Quarterly Review* (Tory). They took books, as the intellectual lifeblood of the nation, very seriously. A decade later, in 1817, the hucksterish publisher Henry Colburn, nicknamed the 'Prince of Puffers', founded his *Literary Gazette*, Britain's first weekly review of books. The *Gazette* was designed to do two things: puff Colburn's own publications and hatchet those of his rival publishers. Colburn took sales very seriously.

These two irreconcileable elements – the high minded and the hard nosed – have jostled uneasily ever since. At one pole is George Steiner – every thinking person's favourite polyglot big brain; at the other what in the American film industry are called 'quote whores' – venal reviewers, so called, whose only function is to fawn or attack on command and for a price.

The plurality, diverse range, high quality and intellectual honesty of book reviewing in London owes everything to its peculiar economics. Unlike other separable sections of the newspaper – sport, business, travel, education – it is rarely written by card-carrying journalists. Reviewing assignments are farmed out as piece work to outside experts, authors and academics – typically not National Union of Journalists members. Without a union or tenure, book reviewers are the cheapest dates in journalism – and the most often jilted.

Occasionally, as with John Carey at the *Sunday Times* or Peter Conrad at the *Observer*, they may be on a retainer in return for exclusive services. But, unlike the paper's movie and theatre reviewers, they will not have their regular weekly slot. You cannot open your paper and know, as with Philip French, senior film reviewer on the *Observer*, that you will find them where they were last week.

Because they are 'casuals', book reviewers incur no overhead costs to the newspaper. They occupy no desk space in the building. They have no computer account. They demand no benefits and run up no expenses. They also have no job security. Average rates of pay range from £150 to £400 for an 800-word review that, with reading and research, can take up to twelve hours' work and a lifetime's accumulated specialist knowledge. Nowhere else on a quality newspaper, other than in the letters page, is white space filled so economically with good writing. Nor need the paymaster feel at all guilty. Most book reviewers are moonlighting – they have day jobs teaching or whatever. Some, for the sheer thrill of seeing their byline in a mass circulation paper, would review for nothing. Some might even pay the newspaper. Reviewers are the coolies of the literary journalism world: and, for those believers in the doctrine 'You get what you pay for', the reviewer's stipend may well explain the quality of the product.

On the plus side, one can trust that the review pages are likely to be more independent-minded than some other, journalistically staffed sections of the paper. But this comes along with a huge minus. Fiction reviews do not cover the field – nowhere near. As was said earlier, no major film or West End theatre production will not have its first night reviews. And those reviews – particularly if they concur – will have a potent effect on the success or failure of the production at the box office. Fewer than 5 per cent of new novels, as I would estimate, get reviewed in mass-market outlets. Another obvious drawback is that only new, hardcover novels are reviewed. Paperback reprints, which are the most bought, even by discriminating readers, tend to slip through the reviewing net. Stage and film revivals, by contrast, do get noticed.

The third, and most serious, drawback is the captiousness of individual reviewers, for whom it is often a matter of professional pride not to agree with each other. Nowhere is the *tot homines, quot sententiae* (so many men, so many minds) rule more evident. The discordance can be bewildering. The LRB's Adam Phillips gave *The Sea* a rave review. On the other side of the net, the TLS's Robert Macfarlane found the novel boring. In *The New York Times*, Michiko Kakutani was savagely dismissive, while the *Boston Globe* (perhaps with an ear better attuned to Irish accentuation) loved Banville's novel.

What should the reader deduce from this? Is the novel worth investing time or money in, or not? In the *Evening Standard*, I declared that *Shalimar the Clown* finds Salman Rushdie, the creator of some of the most sublime prose of our time, 'writing at his best'. In the *Sunday Times*, six days later, Peter Kemp – the reviewer with the sharpest and bloodiest hatchet in London – carves into the novel, labelling Rushdie's prose 'a retirement home for worn-out magic realism cliché' (not something likely to be seen blazoned on the paperback reprint).

It is said that in the 1930s Arnold Bennett, then chief reviewer at the *Evening Standard*, could clear a whole edition of a new novel with a good notice. No single reviewer in Britain or America now has that power (John Carey and Michiko Kakutani are the only possible candidates). None the less, full-blooded butchery can severely lame a novel, if not quite bring it down. Such was the case with Tibor Fischer's critical assault on Martin Amis's *Yellow Dog* in 2003. A Man Booker judge, Fischer had been given a proof copy of Amis's novel and his vituperation was published some time before the novel itself appeared in the shops. The abuse (it could hardly be called literary criticism) was published in the *Daily Telegraph* and widely reprinted, creating less a pre-emptive strike than a kicking to death of a novel in the womb:

> *Yellow Dog* isn't bad as in not very good or slightly disappointing. It's not-knowing-where-to-look bad. I was reading my copy on the Tube and I was terrified someone would look over my shoulder (not only because of the embargo, but because someone might think I was enjoying what was on the page). It's like your favourite uncle being caught in a school playground, masturbating.
>
> The way British publishing works is that you go from not being published no matter how good you are, to being published no matter how bad you are.

Many felt Fischer's comments grossly unfair. They were. But they hung over the novel once it became available to the general public like a bad smell (rotting Fischer?). Somehow that image of the uncle wanking in the schoolyard was unexpungeable.

The American critic Dale Peck, author of *Hatchet Jobs* (2004), argues that reviewing finds its true character in critical GBH such as Fischer's. It represents a return to the prehistoric origins of reviewing in Zoilism – a kind of pelting of pretentious literature with dung, lest the writers get above themselves: it is to the novelist what the gown of humiliation was to the Roman politician – a salutary ordeal. Less grandly, bad reviews are fun, so long as you are not the author. There is, it must be admitted, a kind of furtive blood sport pleasure in seeing a novelist suffering. You read on. Whereas most of us stop reading at the first use of the word 'splendid' or 'marvellous' in a review.

For obvious reasons, the relationship between novelists, the reviewing establishment and critics in general is chronically, and often acutely, edgy. A kind of low-intensity warfare prevails, with outbreaks of savagery. It is partly an ownership issue. Who, other than its creator, is to say what a work of fiction means or is worth? It can take years to write a novel and only a few hours for a critic, or a reviewer rushing for a tight deadline, to trash it. And, of course, there are always those critics like the Ayatollah Khomeini who, not satisfied with trashing the novel, want to go and assassinate the offending novelist as well. As the magazine *Index on Censorship* confirms, there will be at any time some novelist who is in hot water for offending the authorities. Recently, in 2005, the Turkish novelist Orhan Pamuk was hauled into court for daring to presume on his international fame as a writer to utter some home truths about Turkey and the Armenian massacre (genocide) in the First World War. As you read this, it will be some other luckless fictioneer. The father of the novel, Daniel Defoe, spent some time in the stocks; so too will, metaphysically, most of his profession, particularly if they do well.

In *Flaubert's Parrot* Julian Barnes squares his (and Gustave's) account with the critic and don who taught him, Enid Starkie. Chapter six ('Emma Bovary's Eyes') opens scathingly:

> Let me tell you why I hate critics. Not for the normal reason that they're failed creators (they usually aren't; they may be failed critics, but that's another matter); or that they're

> by nature carping, jealous, and vain (they usually aren't; if anything, they might be accused of upgrading the second-rate so that their own fine discriminations thereby appear the rarer). No, the reason I hate critics – well, some of the time – is that they write sentences like this ...

There follow some prime examples of Starkie's Flaubertian fatuity. After several pages of blistering sarcasm and personal invective, Barnes concludes, '*now* you know why I hate critics'. Indeed we do. It is not just academic critics he despises but their higher journalistic cousins, the reviewers. During his promotional tour in the US for his 2005 novel *Arthur and George*, Barnes reiterated what he has elsewhere often said: 'I don't read reviews.' Should we, then? With some wariness, would seem to be the answer.

Postscript

There is another kind of reviewer who wields considerable power in the book trade – the 'expert' employed by publishers to advise on publication. How sound is this, in-house reviewer's judgement? Not infallible, it may be assumed. In January 2006, in a literary critical sting operation, the *Sunday Times* submitted less-than-familiar texts in typescript form by V. S. Naipaul and Doris Lessing to a range of London publishers. Most turned them down as the work of no-hopers on the basis of what their reviewers told them.

chapter 25

Bestsellers

IF THE OPINIONS of reviewers are not to be relied on, what about the opinion of other readers like ourselves, faithfully reflected in the weekly bestseller lists? I rejoice, said Doctor Johnson, to concur with the Common Reader. Why should not we?

It helps, as always, to know something about the machine and how it works. The practice of systematically identifying certain books as noteworthy for the speed and volume of their sales – and nothing else – began with the American monthly magazine the *Bookman* and its enterprising editor, Harry Thurston Peck, in 1895. The earliest recorded use of the noun 'bestseller' is from 1902. In 1912, the American trade magazine *Publisher's Weekly* began issuing a bestseller list. A year later the magazine began dividing bestsellers (customarily ten per week) into fiction and non-fiction – although nowadays the term 'bestseller' automatically evokes a certain kind of novel.

Since 1913, further subdivisions have emerged: notably

hardcover and paperback bestsellers. Examining *Publisher's Weekly* records in 1945, Alice Payne Hackett calculated that the all-time bestseller up to that point in historical time was Charles Monroe Sheldon's Christian epic *In His Steps* (1895), with cumulative sales over sixty years of 8-million plus. The universal blank which Sheldon's name now evokes demonstrates that making it in bestsellerdom does not guarantee literary immortality. Hopefully his reward was in heaven.

Gone with the Wind (1936) clocked up 3.5 million in nine years – boosted, of course, by the efforts of MGM and Clark Gable. Undertaking a similar exercise in 1965, Hackett calculated that Grace Metalious's steamy saga of desperate wifehood in a New England suburb, *Peyton Place* (1956), had sold getting on for 10 million in less than ten years; D.H. Lawrence's newly publishable (since 1959) *Lady Chatterley's Lover* had clocked up 6.3 million, and Harold Robbins's fictionalised, grotesquely sexed-up life of Howard Hughes, *The Carpetbaggers* (1960), came in at 5.5 million. In 1975, Hackett discovered that with the paperback 'revolution' of the late 1960s, further growth occurred. There were now novels like Mario Puzo's *The Godfather* (1969), Peter Blatty's *The Exorcist* (1971) and Erich Segal's *Love Story* (1970) – supersellers which cleared 10 million or more in five years (helped by the fact that they were all made into big budget films). Bestsellers, it seems, are ever better sellers.

In the 1980s and 1990s, despite competition from other media, sales of bestselling novels have continued to rocket – in both hardback and paperback form. In the 1980s, Jean Auel's and Stephen King's novels were routinely brought out in first print runs of a million in the expensive, and many millions in the cheaper forms. Higher pressure sales techniques, with bookstore 'chaining' in the US, and the abolition of the Net

Book Agreement in the UK, the lift given by heavily publicised prizes, 'hype', high-pressure advertising and media tie-ins all combined with the bestseller lists to increase both total volume and single title sales of novels. Over 2003–6, Dan Brown's The Da Vinci Code outsold every previous bestseller, and faster. With the 2006-released film, its sales received a further boost. Not since Hervey Allen's buccaneering historical romance Anthony Adverse dominated the bestseller lists in the mid 1930s has one novel so gripped the reading public for so long.

In Britain, and Europe generally, there had traditionally been fierce resistance to the introduction of bestseller lists. Books, it was felt, did not 'compete' against each other; they coexisted. That some titles outsold others was irrelevant. There was clear cultural danger in that the stampede effect (everyone is reading it, therefore I must read it) crowded out less forceful titles. A low pressure, 'civilised' selling environment was healthier. But the transatlantic pull – 'Americanisation' – was ultimately irresistible. The first reliable charts were introduced in England by the publishing trade magazine the Bookseller and the Sunday Times in the mid 1970s. By the turn of the twenty-first century, British and American practice had, effectively, been assimilated. And, in over 50 per cent of fiction titles, they concur on titles of the day.

Whatever other deductions are to be drawn about bestsellers, it is clear that they are increasingly powerful in preventing consumer demand from being dispersed among the 10,000 or so fiction titles available annually and redirecting that demand on to a manageably tight nucleus of texts (now numbered at between 50 and 100, rather than limited to just ten). Manageable for the reader, manageable for the booktrade. But who, given the choice, wants to be managed?

Choosing one's reading matter is as basic a civic freedom as choosing one's political party, and as much to be cherished.

If you are going to consult the lists (and in my view you should, with certain precautions), it is important to understand how they work. As with popular music, the weekly charts do not merely record sales – they stimulate sales. They are not, that is to say, an inert catalogue: they are a powerful advertisement. So your first, self-protective response should be resistance. You do not want to join the flank-rubbing, or stampeding herd. But the second reaction should be curiosity. Why are so many people reading this novel? Bestsellers, like great personal fortunes, are always worth examining critically. How, exactly, did they pull it off?

Very rarely can a novel be hyped into bestsellerdom. Were that the case, publishers would do it all the time, be even richer than they are and never go broke (as they often do). Sometimes the reasons would seem to be transparently psycho-sociological. The success of Tom Clancy's technothrillers, celebrating American imperial superpotency, coincide historically with Ronald Reagan's presidency. One of Reagan's favourite novels was Clancy's first novel, *The Hunt for Red October* (1984), a work he admired almost as much as the film *Rambo*. Clancy was an honoured guest at the White House and can take some credit for the '600 warship' US programme which was instrumental, via the macho madness of the superpower arms race, in bankrupting and eventually bringing down the Evil Empire. Whether, following the example of his Republican predecessor Lincoln, Reagan shook the hand of Clancy as the 'man who ended a Great (Cold) War' is not recorded. So, too, Jeffrey Archer and Mrs Thatcher – whose favoured, if not favourite, novelist was the author of the 1974 rogue's progress *Not a Penny More, Not a*

Penny Less, a novel whose infantile mercantilist selfishness can be seen to have links with Thatcherite economics.

The decay of ideology after 1989 would seem – on the evidence of the charts – to have inaugurated a trend towards New Age mysticism, religious fiction, fantasies of wizardry and warlockry. A novel like Ayn Rand's *Atlas Shrugged* (1957) is refrigerated, 1950s Cold War anti-Soviet communism. At no period other than its own could it have succeeded. Harry Potter in the late 1990s perhaps filled that gaping hole where religion used to be with cheerful paganism. Asking 'why' something is doing so well, rather than 'what is selling' adds a zest to picking up the book of the day and may even cast some illumination on events of the day. But answers are not always easy to come by. Why did *The Da Vinci Code* outsell all rivals in the first half-decade of the new millennium? Christ knows.

chapter 26

The prize novel

IF THE REVIEWERS are untrustworthy, and the mass of
readers who flock to the bestsellers unthinking, what about
the wise people who sit on the juries of literary prizes? Can they
be trusted to guide Everyreader through the jungle? There are,
demonstrably, readers – many of them – who use such prizes as
reliable signposts to what they should read. Whenever a novel
wins a premier award such as the National Book Award (NBA)
in the United States, the Man Booker in Great Britain, or a
novelist is awarded a Nobel, sales jump, usually meteorically.

Not all prizes have this power over readers. The most
venerable fiction prize in the UK is the James Tait Black,
awarded on the judgement of the Regius Professor of English
at the equally venerable Edinburgh University. The James Tait
Black (JTB) was set up in 1922, the year, all lovers of fiction
will know, in which *Ulysses* was published. The novel which
the JTB regarded as prizeworthy in 1922 was David Garnett's
Lady into Fox – a verdict over which literary history has put a
huge exclamation mark.

The JTB has made better judgements since – not least in 2006 with Ian McEwan's *Saturday*. But its annual decisions are rarely registered by the public, even by booklovers. If you want to stop conversation at a Hampstead dinner party, ask the company which novels won the JTB over the last five years. I would have to look them up myself; and I was once a judge. The Pulitzer is the most venerable fiction prize in the US. My guess is that conversation could be similarly killed at a Manhattan dinner party – although some in the company would be able to name winners of the journalism award.

The NBA, Man Booker, Orange and Whitbread prizes succeed in making headlines, not because their judicial machinery – or even their choices – are superior to those of other prizes, but because they are cannier about the value of PR. They are the prizes that make headlines and headlines make sales and sales make more headlines. It will be interesting to see if the Quills Prize, founded in the US in 2005, takes off in the next few years. It has dedicated itself to Oscar-style glitz – rewarding those books which *really* make it with the mass reading public in the real world. Whether it will have the same impact on the book world as the Academy of Motion Picture Arts and Sciences award does on film remains to be seen.

Despite the fact that prizes are awarded by 'judges' – with the implication that some Olympian set of critical faculties is being brought to bear – the verdicts are inevitably controversial. 'Posh bingo', Julian Barnes has disdainfully called the Booker. Victory, that is, depends on the chemistry (the friendships and enmities, or the prejudice) of the judging panel. It is a literary lottery – Lady Luck's Bedside Books. Neither do other authors mince their words. Chairs of judges, says Colm Toibin (referring, I confess, to me in 2005) 'are chosen for their silliness'. (Silly of me then, Colm, when as chair of judges I voted to give you the Encore Award in 1992 for *The Heather Blazing*. You seemed rather gratified at the time, I recall.)

In December 2005, in an interview with Deborah Solomon of *The New York Times*, Julian Barnes offered another unflattering opinion of the prize committees which, seemed, unaccountably always to pass him over:

> Q: *Arthur and George*, which came out in London last summer, was short-listed for the Booker Prize and then lost out to a novel by John Banville. Was that painful for you?
>
> A: I didn't rate my chances because I didn't look at the other books. I looked at the jury.
>
> Q: Are you saying the judges had something against you?
>
> A: I had a sense, let's say. When I was first shortlisted for the Booker Prize [in 1984], it was for my novel *Flaubert's Parrot*. And afterwards one of the judges came up to me and said, 'I had never heard of Flaubert until I read your novel.' He was a Member of Parliament.

Barnes has little time for dons (see his earlier quoted remarks on the luckless Starkie). But perhaps the Regius Professor of French at Edinburgh University might have made a more enlightened choice in 1984 (although, like the Booker, the Regius Professor of English did not – giving that year's award jointly to J. G. Ballard's *Empire of the Sun* and Angela Carter's *Nights at the Circus*). The un-Flaubertian MP in question – why shouldn't he be put in the stocks and pelted with authorial tomatoes, like me? – was Ted Rowlands, now Baron Rowlands, then Labour MP for Merthyr Tydfil. The winning title in 1984 was Anita Brookner's *Hotel Du Lac*. Doubtless Frenchless Ted thought it was a reference to emulsion paint.

Wounded ego (mine, I mean, not Barnes's) apart, judges are misnamed – suggesting as the term does all the wig-and-bench trappings of a high court. At best they are jury persons; more often, the common readers' delegate – particularly where fiction is concerned. Their success rate in hitting on the novels which posterity subsequently judges to have been the best of the year runs, I estimate, having looked at the last three decades' lists, at around 70 per cent. Not bad, not perfect. It is not the kind of signposting one would want on the motorway, or freeway, but none the less useful guidance for the novel reader.

Fiction prize decisions, I would suggest, should be used in two ways. The long and short lists of the Man Booker, for example, can serve as a kind of superior ('posh') bestseller list, or curriculum. They set parameters – indicating not the best fiction, but that which is 'worth reading'. Manifestly, many readers use the lists in that way. Titles on the long list routinely experience a terrific sales boost as readers try them out. Often, nowadays, reading groups lead the way.

This leads to the most obvious use of the prize-awarding process for the reader – it enables you (challenges you) to test your own judgement against that of the panel. Disagreement can often sharpen your critical judgement. Even outrage.

chapter 27

Book of the film? Film of the book?

NOWADAYS IT IS more often a case of 'You've seen the movie, now read the book' – reversing the advertising slogan from when print was king medium. John Le Carré's *The Constant Gardener*, for example, sold many more copies after the 2005 Ralph Fiennes, Rachel Weisz-starring film than it did on publication four years earlier. But what do the book and the film have in common? Can a film be 'faithful' – or is it an inherently sluttish medium? No film, the stern critic F. R. Leavis decreed, could take on Lawrence's *Women in Love*; it would be an 'abomination'. Ken Russell went ahead and abominated anyway. Not too badly, as it turned out.

After its arrival as a visual raree show, film matured into an exclusively narrative art form, drawing generously from print fiction. D. W. Griffith's *The Birth of a Nation* (1915), a pioneer achievement in early film history, is, for example, an adaptation of Thomas Dixon's unspeakably racist *The Clansman* (1905). Nowhere regarded as a pioneer achievement in fiction, other than in KKK archives, Dixon's novel is still to be found highly recommended on the neo-Nazi National Vanguard bookstore site, along with *The Turner Diaries* and that other masterpiece of White Aryan fiction, *Did Six Million Die?* Dixon was paid a handsome $2,000 by Griffith for the subsidiary rights to his novel – probably the first such payment in the long history of 'movie optioning'.

The century-long relationship between the two narrative media has never been one-way but intricately reciprocal. The film which, as I write, is the number one box office draw in London's West End and L.A.'s Universal City complex is Peter Jackson's *King Kong*. The basic idea of the great ape–little woman epic was conceived by 'King of the Thrillers' Edgar Wallace, of Sanders fame, who died during production. Following the 1936, 1972 and 2005 versions there have been a string of so-called 'novelisations'. Currently it is the Corgi paperback *King Kong* by Anthony Browne, 'from the story conceived by Edgar Wallace and Merian C. Cooper' (a lowly 9,550 on Amazon.co.uk's sales list, as I write). Where is the narrative primarily located – on the page or on the screen? Is it a film novelised, or a novelist's scenario adapted?

It is a nice question which is the most travestied text in the history of film adaptation of the classics. There are, alas, many contenders. In its dream factory days Hollywood did truly disgraceful things to fiction. The end of Sam Goldwyn's *Wuthering Heights* (1939) has a youthful Laurence Olivier (an actor never particularly proud of his legs) and Merle Oberon tripping happily over Penistone Crag – a travesty of Emily Brontë's ambiguous ending, in which a chastened Lockwood visits the local graveyard:

> I sought and soon discovered the three headstones on the slope next the moor – the middle one gray, and half buried

in heath; Edgar Linton's only harmonised by the turf and moss creeping up its foot; Heathcliff's still bare.

I lingered round them under that benign sky, watched the moths fluttering among the heath and harebells, listened to the soft wind breathing through the grass, and wondered how any one could ever imagine unquiet slumbers for the sleepers in that quiet earth.

Unquiet is one thing. Gambolling across the hillside like a couple of sex-crazed spring lambs is quite another.

Even a (British) film one can admire whole-heartedly, David Lean's *Great Expectations* (1946), has Pip in the final scene tearing down the curtains at Satis House to let in the light and open the way to a happy-ever-after future with Estella. Dickens himself had trouble getting the ending right. But in each of the three endings for the novel which he drafted, Miss Havisham's house is a burned wreck and in none of them is future happiness between the lovers in prospect. The novel is permeated with the gloomy hues of the novelist's 'dark' period. When Lean made his film, all of Britain could still remember another kind of dark – the blackout. The world outside the warm, gaily lit picture palace was still blemished with bombsites and hearths, typically, were cold. As it happens, I prefer Lean's 'Let there be light' ending to Dickens's melancholy obscurity. It is unlikely that Dickens would.

There are worse factories than Hollywood's: Josef Goebbels' Ministry of Propaganda, for instance. *Jud Süss* (1925), written by Leon Feuchtwanger, is a sympathetic study of the fortunes of a Jewish banker in eighteenth-century Germany. In 1940, the novel (which in translation had made it into the US bestseller lists) was perverted into a horrific film by the Nazis' state-run film industry, specifically designed to inflame SS units before they went on 'special actions', and to anaesthetise the German population as the Jewish persecution was carried out under their noses. Feuchtwanger, by now a refugee in the US, was no more able to protect his property from the violations perpetrated on it by Goebbels's nightmare factory than the Louvre could protect itself from the depredations of art lover and Reichsmarschal Goering.

In general, the trend of film and television adaptation of fiction has become, over the decades, more sensitive to its source material. The Merchant–Ivory lush versionings of Forster's fiction stand out, as does Scorsese's resplendent 1993 film of the Edith Wharton novel *The Age of Innocence* (1920) and, from the same year Spielberg's bleakly documentary *Schindler's List* (his nonsensical *War of the Worlds* is something else); also Andrew Davies's TV adaptations of the classics (and, in 2006, the 2004 Man Booker winner Alan Hollinghurst's *The Line of Beauty*). A film maker like Francis Coppola can even make a great film out of second-rate Mafio melo like *The Godfather*. There is more credit and glory than shame in Hollywood's recent treatment of its print sources.

None the less, without being Leavisite about it, film rarely does full justice to good fiction. Movies have an apparently incorrigible tendency to sentimentalise, simplify and sog up the source. There are a number of possible explanations. The following two are most frequently cited:

1. Cinema audiences, unlike novel readers, cannot bear too much reality. Pool their respective IQs, and that of the film-watchers would be points lower than an equivalent number of public library readers (both, of course, would be lower than the median score in

Mensa). This is dubious, although flattering to the book lover.

2. The film's visual impact – its shock effect – means that the medium must pull its punches, or be guilty of cultural GBH. More so since the film will, quite likely, have children or other susceptibles in its audience.

There is some evidence for this line of argument arising from the great obscenity debates of the 1970s. Two trials were mounted in the UK (and a number of local prosecutions in the US) in the case of Hubert Selby Jr's novel *Last Exit to Brooklyn*, originally published (partially) in 1964. The novel, as the defence's expert witnesses pointed out, is highly moral, not, as critics alleged, sado-pornographic in its purpose. The title ironically reproduces the traffic sign on the expressway that middle class, novel-reading folk speed by ('Go to Brooklyn? Are you crazy? I don't even like to walk through Washington Square at night'). The novel satirises the negligent indifference with which society views the chronic deprivation and depravity of its slums, projects, ghettoes and estates.

This line of defence cut no ice with the defenders of public morality in the early 1970s. The prosecution's case against *Last Exit* focused unrelentingly (and, initially, very successfully) on the graphically described and unbearably protracted (over three interminable pages) death by gang rape of a prostitute, Tralala:

> soon she passed out and they slapped her a few times and she mumbled and turned her head but they couldn't revive her so they continued to fuck her as she lay unconscious on the seat in the lot and soon they tired of the dead piece and the daisychain broke up and they went

back to Willies the Greeks and the base the kids who were watching and waiting to take a turn took out their disappointment on Tralala and tore her clothes to small scraps put a few cigarettes on her nipples pissed on her jerked on her jammed a broomstick up her snatch then bored they left her among the broken bottles rusty cans and rubble.

Last Exit to Brooklyn was filmed in 1989 under the direction of Uli Edel, who did a workmanlike adaptation. But it was adaptation minus Selby's savagery. In the film, Tralala, played by an ostentatiously unblowsy Jennifer Jason Leigh (who, if indeed a prostitute, could have earned enough in a night to keep herself at the Ritz Carlton for a month) is, as in the novel, multiply violated by the low life of the dockside bar and naval base. But she survives her ordeal, depicted in accelerated, stylised montage, rather than Selby's blow-by-blow realism. Afterwards a little boy, whom Tralala has earlier befriended, gives her his coat, and helps her limp off – to the local rape report unit, presumably. No broomstick. Selby collaborated on the screenplay and has a bit part in Edel's film. Presumably he acquiesced in this soggier version of his novel. Other media, other morals.[29]

There is a third explanation for the generic inadequacy of film when it comes to doing justice to print fiction. Film is narrative in a hurry; it has to cut corners. With, at best, two hours at its ten-frame-a-second disposal it cannot – even with montage, flashback, fast-forwarding and jump-cuts – satisfactorily handle long tracts of time. This liability is compounded by the fact that, even with the technical mastery of the make-up department, it is difficult to get characters to age convincingly.

This last disability creates a small flaw in what was otherwise the most applauded movie of late 2005–early 2006, Brokeback Mountain. A spectacularly counter-conventional story of gay love on the range, the narrative is based on a long short story by E. Annie Proulx, first published in 1997. The adaptation is remarkably faithful – if you allow for a few softened edges. The heroes' relationships with their children is, for example, sentimentalised and enlarged on, presumably for the benefit of the women in the audience. But the opening paragraph of Proulx's story – which has flashed forward to the surviving cowboy lover in old age – pinpoints a breakdown in the film adaptation.

> Ennis del Mar wakes before five, wind rocking the trailer, hissing in around the aluminium door and window frames. The shirts hanging on a nail shudder slightly in the draft. He gets up, scratching the grey wedge of belly and pubic hair, shuffles to the gas burner, pours leftover coffee in a chipped enamel pan; the flame swathes it in blue. He turns on the tap and urinates in the sink, pulls on his shirt and jeans, his worn boots, stamping the heels against the floor to get them full on. The wind booms down the curved length of the trailer and under its roaring passage he can hear the scratching of fine gravel and sand. It could be bad on the highway with the horse trailer. He has to be packed and away from the place that morning.

The film, even with the aid of some drastic jump cutting, cannot persuasively chronicle the passing of four decades from the men's first wild lovemaking as young ranch hands camping out on Brokeback Mountain to the survivor's wholly washed-up old age, contemplating lonely death and the end of his freebooting way of life in a godforsaken Wyoming trailer park. In the corresponding and much less stressed scene in the film, even with cosmetic crows' feet round Ennis's (actor Heath Ledger's) eyes, and an artfully padded jawline, he still looks what he is: a young guy made up to look old(ish). You can be sure that, underneath the jeans, the make-up people did not dye his belly and pubic hair grey. Admittedly it is better than what was done with James Dean in the final scenes of the 1956 film adaptation of Edna Ferber's *Giant*. But this kind of effect never works on screen as effectively as it works on page.

I, like many others, read the Proulx short story after seeing the film. Films, even films that do not work as well as *Brokeback Mountain*, can serve as useful gateways to fiction – especially demanding fiction. It helps get into the book version of Henry James's *The Wings of the Dove* (1902) or *The Golden Bowl* (1904) – two of the more demanding novels in the canon – to have seen the 1997 and 2000 films first.

But here, too, you should be careful. One of the disadvantages of viewing, or previewing, a screen (film or TV) version of a novel, particularly a classic novel, is that it can 'fix' your mental imagery too rigidly – infringe your privilege as reader of casting the parts, setting the scene and playing out the narrative yourself.

Who, for example, when embarking on their annual reading of *Pride and Prejudice* (a refreshing practice, strongly recommended by the Jane Austen Society) wants, every year, to have the nipples and wet shirt of Colin Firth intruding between them and the picture of Darcy evoked by the text? Who, to invoke Leavis's anathema again, wants the mental image of Oliver Reed's and Alan Bates's virile members flapping around the page as they read the 'Blutbrüderschaft' chapter in Women in Love?

The point was made forcibly by Philip Hensher, explaining in the Guardian why, however excellent and applauded Andrew Davies's 2005 adaptation of Bleak House might be, he, Hensher, would not watch it – on critical principle:

> But the main reason for not wanting to watch this Bleak House is simply that one doesn't want it in one's head. I don't want forever to have to think of Gillian Anderson when I get to Lady Dedlock, and certainly not of Johnny Vegas as Krook. How many novels have been subtly corrupted in the imagination like this? Certainly, I can't read Brideshead Revisited without seeing Anthony Andrews and Jeremy Irons, and Julia Sawalha has a most disconcerting habit of intruding on a reading of Pride and Prejudice. The better the dramatisation, the worse the danger that another imagination will interpose itself between the author's and the reader's; one nothing to do with either.[30]

Few, I suspect, will impose on themselves Hensher's nobly self-denying ordinance. It has overtones of Jack D. Ripper's fanatic reverence for Purity of Essence. Does Hensher, I wonder, read from a sterilised copy of Bleak House, with Phiz's 'subtly corrupting' illustrations ripped out? But the point is worth bearing in mind. Film adaptations can stimulate, they can enlighten, but they can also rigidly format one's sense of the printed original.

chapter 28

After all is said and done, what use are they?

GRAND CLAIMS HAVE been made for the novel – none grander than that of D. H. Lawrence, for whom it was 'the one bright book of life'. The Bible, that is, for (in the UK, at least) a post-biblical age. Few works of fiction can match up to Lawrence's exalted definition. Not even, possibly, all of Lawrence's fiction.

Nowhere less than in fiction, however, does one critical description fit all. For some, at the other extreme from Lawrence, the novel has been the one bright book of death. It is plausibly argued, for example, that Graham Young, the UK's most notorious mass poisoner, celebrated in the 1995 film *The Young Poisoner's Handbook*, was inspired in his use of the 'undetectable' poison, thallium, by Agatha Christie's novel *The Pale Horse* (1961). Her innocently conceived mystery novel was the Young Poisoner's Manual. As has been noted earlier, Timothy McVeigh, perpetrator of the worst civilian atrocity in American history, took his inspiration (and, as regards the explosive properties of ammonium nitrate farm fertiliser, his technical instruction) from, *The Turner Diaries*.

Less homicidal readers than Young and McVeigh have found novels to be useful manuals. In late December 2005 British government documents of thirty years earlier were declassified. Prominent among these were those related to the case of John Stonehouse, the MP who in 1974 faked his death – 'Did a Reginald Perrin', in the phrase of the day – and embarked on a new life in Australia as 'Joseph Markham' with his mistress Sheila Buckley ('Mrs M'). Stonehouse had created a new identity for himself from the instructions offered in Frederick Forsyth's 1971 thriller *The Day of the Jackal*. The now notorious paragraph in the novel beginning 'there is nothing easier than getting a false passport' has been drawn on time and again over the decades, by IRA cells and whole armies of illegal immigrants, by benefits fraudsters and – most recently – 'phisers', identity thieves. Apparently Forsyth himself has instructed the Home Office how they might close the 'Jackal loophole', but without success. It remains gapingly open.

For the law-abiding, fiction also has its manifold practical uses. In the nineteenth century, the period of its most rapid hot-house growth, the novel developed, as one of its many parts, into a middle-class manual of conduct. Anthony Trollope, when asked what good his novels did society, liked to reply that they instructed maidens how they should receive their suitors. Jane Austen's novels (like those of her literary descendant, Helen Fielding of *Bridget Jones's Diaries* (1996) fame) are similarly instructional about the big question in a young woman's life: whom should I marry? A Mr Collins, a Mr Darcy or no one? Mr Elton, Mr Churchill, Mr Knightley or no one? Edmund, Henry or no one?

Miss Austen, having accepted her suitor, decided – after a

night's second thoughts on the matter – that it would, after all, be no one. One would like to think that having chewed the issues over so thoroughly in her novels helped her to the decision. Oddly, none of her heroines opts for spinsterhood, and those that are left on the shelf, like Miss Bates, are no advertisement for the single woman past her 'bloom' – that disaster which faces Anne Elliot. For a woman, said Jacqueline Susann (not, like Fielding, one of Jane's more distinguished literary descendants), 'forty is Hiroshima'. Miss Austen would have agreed, but, on the evidence of *Persuasion*, would have located the catastrophe at twenty-seven. Bridget Jones, I daresay, at thirty-three (next year, always next year).

It is unfashionable to assert it, but the novel does, I believe, still have a socio-educational value. It is not just Miss Manners. Fiction can make us better, or at least, better informed citizens. In a technological age, for example, it is important that the population should know something about how the machinery that makes modern life possible works. Science fiction has done as much for the factual scientific education of the average reader as all the educational reforms introduced since C. P. Snow's 1959 polemic *The Two Cultures* lamented his fellow Britons' epidemic ignorance of the second law of thermodynamics. The fact, revealed in a survey by the magazine *Wired* in November 2005, that 40 per cent of Americans none the less believe that aliens are in the habit of routinely visiting our planet and taking away sample earthlings for full body cavity probes, suggests that sf may also have a lot to answer for in the dumbing down of the citizenry. But, on the whole, the genre has, I believe, made us more knowledgeable.

Michael Crichton's career is a prime example for those, like myself, who want to believe that sf wises up more than it dumbs down. Crichton's *The Andromeda Strain* was the first true title in the genre to make it to number one on *The New York Times* bestseller list in 1969. The novel's breakthrough success is attributable to the fact that its descriptions of space hardware (what computers do, for example) made the concurrent moon landings comprehensible to the American population. Crichton's vastly successful *Jurassic Park* (1990) later introduced a whole generation, via the beloved dinosaur, to the intricacies of Crick and Watson's Nobel-winning discoveries about DNA and the complexities of chaos theory (something that Spielberg prudently left out of the film version).

How much we can trust fiction, even fiction as laboriously researched as Michael Crichton's, to be our educator remains a moot question. On the strength of his 2004 number one bestseller, *State of Fear*, the novelist was invited to testify in 2005 before a US Senate committee investigating climate change. *State of Fear* is a 'pulse-pounding' techno-thriller based on the premise that the greenhouse gas thesis is a gigantic scam – what Crichton in his appended 'message' (ballasted by a voluminous bibliography) calls 'politicised science'. It is, Crichton believes, as fallacious as was eugenics in the early nineteenth century and alchemy in the seventeenth. And dangerous. The politicians and oil barons love him.

Crichton's epigraph, from Orwell, signals that he conceives *State of Fear* as a message to the sadly unenlightened planet:

> Within any important issue, there are always aspects no one wants to discuss.

Except, of course, the intrepid novelist.

Crichton is unusual in being a novelist with degrees in

medicine from Harvard. Why, then, wouldn't he know more about things scientific than some blowhard columnist in the *Independent* whose expertise about meteorology is confined to watching Sian Lloyd's weather reports? The fact is, no one knows how accurate what Crichton knows, or thinks he knows, is. Crichton is as likely to be wrong about climate change as he was about the imminent Japanese takeover of America, as outlined in his 'Wake up, America!' novel, *Rising Sun*. Shortly after the novel's publication, the Tokyo real estate market collapsed and the Japanese economy became a basket case – no more a yellow peril threat to the USA than Fiji.

Readers can still enjoy *State of Fear*, whether they go along with Crichton or not. And, whatever else, those who get through the book will probably know more about the issues than they did before and may even be stimulated to find out yet more. This kind of clueing up ('education' is too grand term) can be found in much fiction which is read, primarily, for enjoyment or distraction. Arthur Hailey, for example, built a bestselling career on novels that explained to the averagely uninformed citizen how modern travel works (*Airport* (1968)), how Detroit produces automobiles (*Wheels* (1971)), how banks make their money and look after ours (*The Moneychangers* (1975)), how the American electrical grid works (*Overload* (1979)). Hailey's 'researched' fiction, which consistently made the number one spot in the 1960s and 1970s, left its reader more knowledgeable as well as entertained (there must have been a special piquancy reading *Airport* in the airport departure lounge). Trollope would have approved, although the one thing that Hailey's info-fiction does not help with is how maidens should receive their gentleman admirers.

Coming to the present, and plucking a couple of examples at random from the early 2006 shelves, an excellent analysis of Chernobyl, and the dangers of nuclear-generated fuel, is given in Martin Cruz Smith's latest Arkady ('Gorky Park') Renko thriller, *Wolves Eat Dogs* (2004). Against the backdrop of cases such as that of reformed murderer 'Tookie' Williams – something that may cost Governor Schwarzenegger dear at the next election – an intricate exposition of the California appellate court system as it affects death row inmates makes up the plot of Richard North Patterson's *Conviction* (2005). Both these are main-course airport novels (I bought them at Heathrow, to while away the eleven-hour journey to LAX). But, beneath the thrillerish sugar coating, they are informational. I put them down knowing more than I did before about what is making headlines and, arguably, current history.

Novels can do many things. They can instruct, enlighten, confuse, mislead, soothe, excite, indoctrinate, misinform, educate and waste time. Each novel has its own rewards, or frustrations. And, at their highest pitch of achievement, novels can indeed be the one bright book of life. The trick is finding which, among the millions now accessible, fits that bill. For you, that is. And that, as Virginia Woolf told us, is something no one can tell you. Or, if they do, ignore them.

Afterword

ROBINSON CRUSOE, marooned on his island all those years, had no novels to read other than the one which he (with the invisible assistance of Daniel Defoe) wrote himself. Castaways on the radio programme *Desert Island Discs* have it easier. Among other comforts they are allowed eight gramophone records. In the early days, when the programme was still conducted by its originator, Roy Plomley, the castaway was allowed an 'endless supply of needles', which has a Crusoe-like sound to it. Now it is fancifully assumed that the island has an endless supply of electricity for the iPod, doubtless energised by a solar panel.

The castaway is also, having sorted out the music, charged with choosing the one book they would like to take with them, to console the lonely rest of their life – other, of course, than the Bible and the works of Shakespeare (not because those treasures grow on trees, but to forestall repetitive choice).

When, mysteriously, I was invited on the programme and asked to choose the 'book' I went for Thackeray's *Vanity Fair*. I was amused the following week when the philosopher Alain de Botton, in one of the snappy Q&A interviews now popular in newspapers, cited Thackeray's book as 'the most over-rated ever'.

I have no doubt that both points of view can be plausibly sustained. Novels, as has been said repeatedly in the previous pages, can provoke as different responses as people themselves are different. What is interesting is why, in any particular case, the response is provoked.

I cannot speak for de Botton, but *Vanity Fair* is where it is on my list for at least three reasons. I have very warm feelings about how I first came across the novel. The first Victorian novel I read, aged nine, was *Masterman Ready* (1841) by Frederick Marryat. It was a set school book. During the Second World War, a period of acute shortage, texts designed for children of long previous eras continued to circulate in the classroom. Marryat's nautical tale was designed to instill ideals of manliness and maidenhood in young Victorian scholars. I cannot speak for the manliness, but the novel indoctrinated me with an affection for nineteenth-century fiction which I have never lost. Among novels which I read before passing the Eleven-plus were George du Maurier's *Trilby* (1894), Charles Kingsley's *Westward Ho!* (1855) and Richard Doddridge Blackmore's *Lorna Doone* (1869) (a novel whose description of the 'great winter of 1683' was vividly appropriate for a child who had shivered through the great winter of 1947).

What Marryat, du Maurier, Blackmore and Kingsley had in common was an acknowledged affiliation to Thackeray, and his easy-going, digressive mode of narration. The author of *Vanity Fair* himself – although I had read quite widely by then the 'lesser Thackeray', Trollope – I did not seriously encounter until my first year in university. I had been put off, while still a schoolboy, by a somewhat baffled attempt at *The Virginians* (1857–9) (not merely the worst novel Thackeray ever wrote, but the worst novel *anyone* ever wrote, as one Victorian wag put it. Bad enough for me).

I was introduced to *Vanity Fair* by my tutor, Monica Jones – a woman best known to posterity as the paramour, and occasional muse, of Philip Larkin. Thackeray and Scott, Jones assured me, would be 'gold in your pocket for life'. Which they were. Thackeray's 'cynical' (more Sterneian than Swiftian) attitude, his easy worldliness and, above all, his eloquent, ever-flowing conversational mode of narrative fitted my desultory reading habits like hand and glove. I bought a second-hand Smith Elder *Centenary Biographical Edition* of the complete works (at two shillings a volume – the set now goes for £700) and read through them – even the worst ever *The Virginians*. A PhD and monograph (*Thackeray at Work*) followed, along with editions of several of the major works.

Sadly, the power of those earlier, pre-Thackerayan experiences has faded. I can read neither Kingsley (Henry, perhaps better than Charles) with pleasure, nor Marryat. When, not having re-read the novel for thirty years, I took on *Lorna Doone* as an editing chore I was dismayed to find that reading Blackmore's turgid prose was like chewing sawdust. The magic had gone. There is not that much time left me now (certainly not another thirty years) and it may be the magic of *Vanity Fair* will bleed away. But I doubt it.

The novel was right for me. It was obviously anything but right for de Botton – or perhaps he has a superior critical sensibility which, more correctly than mine, judges Thackeray inferior. I hope not. I hope that our divergent preferences are attributable to the fortunes of personal reading history. Right or wrong as my judgments may be, my experiences have been very happy for me. And it is that happiness which, I would argue, justifies the large investments of time, effort and even money which the novel requires. They are, I believe, well worth it.

Notes

1. For the deduction that Anna is reading Trollope, see John Sutherland, *Who Betrays Elizabeth Bennet?* (Oxford University Press, 1999).

2. The esteemed American literary critic Lionel Trilling, like his British counterpart F. R. Leavis, was a great maker of fiction curricula for the self-improving undergraduate. See his influential treatise *The Liberal Imagination* (Viking Press, 1950).

3. Oddly, the best critics – such as Trilling (above) – often write rather less than excellent novels. See, for example, Trilling's melodrama of liberal conscience during the McCarthy years, *The Middle of the Journey* (1947).

4. For a convenient selection of, and guide to, Woolf's highly opinionated reviews, see <u>http://etext.library.adelaide.edu.au/w/woolf/virginia/</u>.

5. Also worth looking at is Uris's *QBVII*, a novel which bravely courted libel proceedings by 'outing' a Nazi concentration camp doctor. He duly sued and, after proceedings in the courtroom indicated by the title, the former Nazi was awarded a derisory half-penny damages.

6. One of the Provo internees, Brighton Bomber Patrick Magee, wrote a PhD on the Troubles as reflected in popular fiction. The

thesis was later published as *Gangsters or Guerrillas?* (Beyond the Pale, 2001).

7. £1.35, I think.

8. See www.media.mit.edu/micromedia/elecpaper.html.

9. In his book about Diderot's world-changing encyclopaedia, *The Business of Enlightenment* (Princeton, 1979).

10. See, for example, Julian Barnes below, p. 232.

11. Alan Turing in 1947, quoted in Andrew Hodge, *Alan Turing: The Enigma* (1983).

12. The amount Wylie secured – something under half a million pounds for a three-book, six-year deal – is considerably less than a QC or the CEO of any large business organisation might expect. The author's purse is so traditionally empty that even a moderate amount can seem like a fortune.

13. See chapter 26 The Prize Novel.

14. For more on genre fiction, see pp. 139–51.

15. Following the mid-1960s feminist revolution, *Lady Chatterley's Lover* has, ironically, by virtue of its author's ineradicable male chauvinism, been re-entered in the Index of Prohibited Books – at least in feminist circles.

16. Or three contexts – I remember the impact the novel had on me when I first read it in the 1960s and the technology was still grippingly plausible.

17. The argument is found in Benjamin's essay on Nikolai Leskov, collected in *Illuminations*, ed. Hannah Arendt, trans. Harry Zohn (Harcourt, Brace and World, 1968).

18. 'Far from the madding crowd's ignoble strife,
    Their sober wishes never learn'd to stray;

> Along the cool sequester'd vale of life
> They kept the noiseless tenor of their way.'

19. In the depraved (as they fondly thought) 1970s, the one remaining subject which was deemed to be 'beyond a joke' was dead babies. Inevitably, it being a decade of rebellion, jokes were made. In the noughties, there are whole websites devoted to dead baby jokes. When it was first published in the United States, the title of Amis's novel was changed to *Dark Secrets* to avoid upsetting sensibilities.

20. William Sharp (1855–1905) maintained through life that this Celtic Fringe novelist was real – and his cousin. He even confected an entry for her in *Who's Who*. 'Her' fiction is generally regarded as being more interesting and vital than her creator's.

21. This immensely complicated topic is discussed authoritatively in a special edition of the magazine *Modernism/ Modernity* (April 2006), devoted to 'Modernism and Film'.

22. There is one of him, allegedly taken when he was a sailor in 1957, posted on <u>wikipedia.com</u>.

23. Kristeva's term was widely popularised by Roland Barthes's use and elaboration of it in his criticism.

24. Mudie originally had a bookshop near the newly established London University (now University College London) in Bloomsbury. He got royally fed up with students coming in, reading his books and leaving without buying anything. Now Waterstone's, by UCL, discourages overlength browsing with a threatening cohort of 'security personnel'.

25. I have used this example before, in *Victorian Fiction, Novelists, Publishers and Readers* (Macmillan, 1994).

26. None the less, theoretical physicists' 1990s hypothesis about 'worm holes' in the fabric of time legitimised fantasies such as Michael Crichton's *Timeline* (1999). Fred Hoyle, the British astronomer, wrote numerous novels, such as *The Black Cloud* (1957), popularising his scientific research as to the origins of life in the universe.

27. It may be familiar from the 1982 film *Poltergeist*, which was inspired by an actual event in which coffins in a cemetery around the Verdugo (the word means hangman) hills, near La Cañada, surfaced and started floating away during a fierce downpour.

28. 'Blogcrit' is, of course, advancing fast. A google on the term will call up dozens of sites.

29. The film adaptation of another Selby novel, *Requiem for a Dream* (1978), was more faithful. (Selby had a bit part in that movie as well.) But again the film-makers could not resist making the novel's two absolutely strung-out druggies, played by Jared Leto and Marlon Wayans, even in the depths of their addictive hell, as attractive as GQ models.

30. Hensher's remarks mightily peeved Andrew Davies, who responded angrily in the letter columns of the *Guardian*.

List of illustrations

Acknowledgements

I AM VERY grateful to John Davey, for his careful (and expert) advice and (equally expert) corrections. I hope I shall not have let him down with the errors which doubtless remain. I am grateful to Sarah M. Lee for assistance with the preparation of the illustrations. Much of the work for this book was done, teaching, at UCL and Caltech. The very best way to read (and certainly to enjoy) novels, I would maintain, is with others. It's a privilege for me to have done so, and with so many clever young minds.

Bibliography

Novels cited, quoted, or discussed in the text (by title, alphabetically, dates of first publication only)

2001: A Space Odyssey (1968) Arthur C. Clarke

The Accidental (2005) Ali Smith
Across the River and into the Trees (1952) Ernest Hemingway
The Age of Innocence (1920) Edith Wharton
The Alteration (1976) Kingley Amis
After Many a Summer (1939) Aldous Huxley
Airport (1968) Arthur Hailey
An American Dream (1965) Norman Mailer
American Psycho (1991) Bret Easton Ellis
An American Tragedy (1925) Theodore Dreiser
The Andromeda Strain (1969) Michael Crichton
Angelica's Grotto (1999) Russell Hoban
Animal Farm (1945) George Orwell
Anna Karenina (1877, trans. David Magarshack, 2005) Leo
    Tolstoy
Antic Hay (1923) Aldous Huxley
Arthur and George (2005) Julian Barnes

Ashenden (1928) W. Somerset Maugham

Atlas Shrugged (1957) Ayn Rand

Atomised (1998, trans. Frank Wynne, 2000) Michel
   Houellebecq

The Awakening (1899) Kate Chopin

Battle Cry (1953) Leon Uris

The Battle of Dorking (1871) Colonel G. T. Chesney

Beasts of No Nation (2005) Uzodinma Iweala

Berlin Alexanderplatz (1929) Alfred Döblin

Between the Acts (1941) Virginia Woolf

The Bell Jar (1963) Sylvia Plath

Beloved (1987) Toni Morrison

Birdsong (1993) Sebastian Faulks

Black Beauty (1877) Anna Sewell

The Black Cloud (1957) Fred Hoyle

Bleak House (1852) Charles Dickens

The Bonfire of the Vanities (1987) Tom Wolfe

Bonjour Tristesse (1953) Françoise Sagan

Brave New World (1932) Aldous Huxley

Brick Lane (2003) Monica Ali

Brideshead Revisited (1945) Evelyn Waugh

Bridget Jones's Diaries (1996) Helen Fielding

Brighton Rock (1938) Graham Greene

Bring the Jubilee (1953) Ward Moore

The British Museum is Falling Down (1965) David Lodge

Brokeback Mountain (1997) E. Annie Proulx

The Buddha of Suburbia (1990) Hanif Kureishi

Caleb Williams (1794) William Godwin

Cancer Ward (1968) Alexander Solzhenitsyn

Candide (1759) Voltaire

Candy (1958) Terry Southern

The Carpetbaggers (1960) Harold Robbins

A Christmas Carol (1843) Charles Dickens

City of Spades (1957) Colin MacInnes

The Clansman (1905) Thomas Dixon

Clarissa (1748) Samuel Richardson

A Clockwork Orange (1962) Anthony Burgess

Cocaine Nights (1997) J. G. Ballard

The Comedians (1965) Graham Greene

The Coming Race (1871) Edward Bulwer-Lytton

The Constant Gardener (2001) John Le Carré

Conviction (2005) Richard North Patterson

Crash (1973) J. G. Ballard

Crime and Punishment (1866, trans. C. J. Coulson 1981) Fyodor
    Dostoevsky

Crome Yellow (1921) Aldous Huxley

Cry, the Beloved Country (1948) Alan Paton

The Crying of Lot 49 (1966) Thomas Pynchon

Cujo (1981) Stephen King

The Da Vinci Code (2003) Dan Brown

Dancing in the Dark (2005) Caryl Phillips

The Day of the Jackal (1971) Frederick Forsyth

Dead Babies (1975) Martin Amis

Destry Rides Again (1930) Max Brand

Disgrace (1999) J. M. Coetzee

Do Androids Dream of Electronic Sheep? (1968) Philip K. Dick

Dombey and Son (1848) Charles Dickens

Dr No (1962) Ian Fleming

Dreamcatcher (2000) Stephen King

The Drowned World (1962) J. G. Ballard

Dust Tracks on a Road (1924) Zora Neale Hurston

The Eiger Sanction (1972) 'Trevanian' (Rodney Whitaker)
Emma (1816) Jane Austen
Empire of the Sun (1984) J. G. Ballard
The End of the Affair (1957) Graham Greene
The End of Alice (1996) A. M. Homes
Enduring Love (1997) Ian McEwan
England Made Me (1935) Graham Greene
Everything is Illuminated (2002) Jonathan Safran Foer
The Exorcist (1971) Peter Blatty
The Eye of the World (1990) Robert Jordan
Eyeless in Gaza (1936) Aldous Huxley

Fahrenheit 451 (1953) Ray Bradbury
Far from the Madding Crowd (1874) Thomas Hardy
Fatherland (1992) Robert Harris
Fever Pitch (1992) Nick Hornby
Finnegans Wake (1939) James Joyce
Firestarter (1980) Stephen King
The Firm (1991) John Grisham
The First Casualty (2005) Will Self
The Fit (2004) Philip Hensher
The Fixer (1967) Bernard Malamud
Flashman (1969) George Macdonald Fraser
Flaubert's Parrot (1984) Julian Barnes
For Whom the Bell Tolls (1940) Ernest Hemingway
Frankenstein (1818) Mary Shelley
From Russia with Love (1963) Ian Fleming

Giant (1952) Edna Ferber
The Godfather (1969) Mario Puzo
The Golden Bowl (1904) Henry James
Gone with the Wind (1936) Margaret Mitchell

Goodbye, Columbus (1959) Philip Roth
The Good Earth (1931) Pearl S. Buck
Great Expectations (1861) Charles Dickens
The Great Fire of London (1982) Peter Ackroyd
The Great Gatsby (1925) F. Scott Fitzgerald
The Green Man (1969) Kingsley Amis
The Group (1963) Mary McCarthy
The Groves of Academe (1952) Mary McCarthy
Gulliver's Travels (1726) Jonathan Swift

A Handful of Dust (1934) Evelyn Waugh
The Hand-Reared Boy (1970) Brian Aldiss
Harry Potter and the Half-Blood Prince (2005) J. K. Rowling
The Heart of the Matter (1948) Graham Greene
The Heather Blazing (1992) Colm Toibin
High Fidelity (1995) Nick Hornby
The History Man (1975) Malcolm Bradbury
Hotel du Lac (1984) Anita Brookner
The Hours (1998) Michael Cunningham
Howards End (1910) E. M. Forster
The Human Stain (2000) Philip Roth
Humphry Clinker (1771) T. Smollett
The Hunt for Red October (1984) Tom Clancy
Hunter (1989) William M. Pierce

Is He Popenjoy? (1878) Anthony Trollope
The Italian (1797) Ann Radcliffe
Ivanhoe (1819) Walter Scott

Jane Eyre (1847) Charlotte Brontë
John Halifax Gentleman (1856) Mrs Dinah Craik
Jud Süss (1925) Leon Feuchtwanger

Jurassic Park (1990) Michael Crichton

Kenilworth (1821) Walter Scott
Knife of Dreams (2005) Robert Jordan

Lady Audley's Secret (1862) Mary E. Braddon
Lady Chatterley's Lover (1928) D. H. Lawrence
Last Exit to Brooklyn (1964) Hubert Selby Jr
Left Behind (1995) Tim LaHaye and Jerry B. Jenkins
Less than Zero (1985) Bret Easton Ellis
The Lincoln Lawyer (2005) Michael Connelly
The Line of Beauty (2004) Alan Hollinghurst
Lolita (1955) Vladimir Nabokov
The Long Firm (1999) Jake Arnott
A Long Way Down (2005) Nick Hornby
Lorna Doone (1869) R. D. Blackmore
Love Story (1970) Erich Segal
Lucky Jim (1954) Kingsley Amis
Lunar Park (2005) Bret Easton Ellis

Madame Bovary (1857) Gustave Flaubert
Malaeska (1860) Ann S. Stephens
A Man in Full (1998) Tom Wolfe
The Man in the High Castle (1962) Philip K. Dick
Marcella (1894) Mrs Humphry Ward
The March (2005) E. L. Doctorow
Martin Lukes: Who Moved my Blackberry (2005) Lucy Kellaway
Masterman Ready (1841) Frederick Marryat
Memorias de mis Putas Tristes (2004) Gabriel Garcia Márquez
Middle of the Journey (1947) Lionel Trilling
Middlemarch (1872) George Eliot
Midnight's Children (1981) Salman Rushdie

Moby-Dick (1851) Herman Melville
Money (1984) Martin Amis
The Moneychangers (1975) Arthur Hailey
The Moonstone (1868) Wilkie Collins
Mrs Dalloway (1925) Virginia Woolf
Murder in Byzantium (2006) Julia Kristeva
Murder on the Orient Express (1934) Agatha Christie
My Brilliant Career (1901) Miles Franklin
The Mysteries of Udolpho (1794) Ann Radcliffe

The Naked and the Dead (1947) Norman Mailer
The Name of the Rose (1983) Umberto Eco
The Natural (1952) Bernard Malamud
Night Train (1997) Martin Amis
Nights at the Circus (1984) Angela Carter
Nineteen Eighty-Four (1949) George Orwell
Northanger Abbey (1813) Jane Austen
Not a Penny More, Not a Penny Less (1974) Jeffrey Archer

Oblomov (1858, trans. David Magarshack 2005) Ivan
    Goncharov
On Beauty (2005) Zadie Smith
The Old Man and the Sea (1952) Ernest Hemingway
Oranges are Not the Only Fruit (1985) Jeanette Winterson
Overload (1979) Arthur Hailey

The Pale Horse (1961) Agatha Christie
Pamela (1740) Samuel Richardson
A Passage to India (1924) E. M. Forster
The People's Act of Love (2005) James Meek
Peyton Place (1956) Grace Metalious
The Pilgrim's Progress (1678) John Bunyan

The Plague (1947, trans. Stuart Gilbert 1991) Albert Camus
The Plot Against America (2005) Philip Roth
Portnoy's Complaint (1969) Philip Roth
Pride and Prejudice (1813) Jane Austen
Primary Colors (1996) Joe Klein

QB VII (1970) Leon Uris

Rebecca (1938) Daphne Du Maurier
The Red Notebook (1995) Paul Auster
Regeneration (1990) Pat Barker
Requiem for a Dream (1978) Hubert Selby Jr
The Riddle of the Sands (1903) Erskine Childers
Riders of the Purple Sage (1912) Zane Grey
The Rings of Saturn (1998) W. G. Sebald
Rising Sun (1992) Michael Crichton
The Riverside Villas Murder (1973) Kingsley Amis
Robinson Crusoe (1719) Daniel Defoe
Room at the Top (1954) John Braine

The Sands of Mars (1951) Arthur C. Clarke
Sanders of the River (1910) Edgar Wallace
Sarrasine (1830) Honoré de Balzac
The Satanic Verses (1988) Salman Rushdie
Saturday (2005) Ian McEwan
Schindler's Ark (1982) Thomas Keneally
The Sea (2005) John Banville
The Sea, The Sea (1978) Iris Murdoch
The Secret Agent (1907) Joseph Conrad
A Secret Service (1892) William Le Queux
Shalimar the Clown (2005) Salman Rushdie
The Sign of Four (1890) Arthur Conan Doyle

The Silence of the Lambs (1988) Thomas Harris
Sin City, vols 1 and 2 (2005) Frank Miller
Skipping Christmas (2001) John Grisham
Slow Man (2005) J. M. Coetzee
Small Island (2004) Andrea Levy
So Long and Thanks for All the Fish (1984) Douglas Adams
The Spy who Came in from the Cold (1963) John le Carré
SS-GB (1978) Len Deighton
Starship (1958) Brian Aldiss
State of Fear (2004) Michael Crichton
The Story of O (1954) Pauline Réage
Summer Crossing (2005) Truman Capote

A Tale of Two Cities (1859) Charles Dickens
This Gun for Hire (1936) Graham Greene
Time and Fate (2005) Lance Price
The Time Machine (1898) H. G. Wells
Time's Arrow (1991) Martin Amis
Timeline (1999) Michael Crichton
To the Lighthouse (1927) Virginia Woolf
Tom Brown's Schooldays (1857) Thomas Hughes
Tom Jones (1749) Henry Fielding
Toxic Bachelors (2005) Danielle Steel
The Treasure of the Sierra Madre (1934) B. Traven
Trilby (1894) George du Maurier
Trinity (1976) Leon Uris
The Turner Diaries (1978) William L. Pierce

Ulysses (1922) James Joyce
Uncle Tom's Cabin (1851) Harriet Beecher Stowe

Vanity Fair (1848) W. M Thackeray

The Virginians (1859) W. M. Thackeray
The Volcano Lovers (1992) Susan Sontag

War and Peace (1869, trans. Anthony Briggs 2006) Leo Tolstoy
The War of the Worlds (1897) H. G. Wells
The Wasp Factory (1984) Iain Banks
Waverley (1814) Walter Scott
Weir of Hermiston (1896) R. L. Stevenson
Westward Ho! (1855) Charles Kingsley
What Maisie Knew (1897) Henry James
What will he Do with It? (1859) Edward Bulwer Lytton
Wheels (1971) Arthur Hailey
White City Blue (1999) Tim Lott
White Teeth (2000) Zadie Smith
The Wind Done Gone (2001) Alice Randall
The Wings of the Dove (1902) Henry James
Wolves Eat Dogs (2004) Martin Cruz Smith
The Woman in White (1860) Wilkie Collins
Women in Love (1920) D. H. Lawrence
Wuthering Heights (1847) Emily Brontë

Yellow Dog (2003) Martin Amis